THE TRUTH SINGS IN CIRCLES
The Trail of the Black Madonna

THE TRUTH SINGS IN CIRCLES

The Trail of the Black Madonna

Mano Warren

ATHENA PRESS
LONDON

THE TRUTH SINGS IN CIRCLES
The Trail of the Black Madonna
Copyright © Mano Warren 2005

All Rights Reserved

No part of this book may be reproduced in any form
by photocopying or by any electronic or mechanical means,
including information storage and retrieval systems,
without permission in writing from both the copyright
owner and the publisher of this book.

ISBN 1 84401 514 9

First Published 2005 by
ATHENA PRESS
Queen's House, 2 Holly Road
Twickenham TW1 4EG
United Kingdom

Printed for Athena Press

Contents

Introduction: The Trail of the Black Madonna, 7

I. Threading the Beads of Myth and Symbol, 15

II. The Story of Isis, Osiris and Horus, 23

III. The Teachings of Isis, a Black Madonna, 30

IV. The Mystery of the Underworld Initiation, 38

V. The Forgotten Knowledge of the Four Elements, 44

VI. Chrétien's Story of Perceval and the Holy Grail, 50

VII. The Message of the Grail, 67

VIII. The Alchemy of the Four Elements in the Psyche, 125

IX. Inanna's Journey into the Underworld, 133

X. Inanna's Keys to the Underworld, 138

Introduction:
The Trail of the Black Madonna

MODERN, WESTERN CULTURES ARE BECOMING HIGHLY out of balance in relation to the rhythms of the earth, and, to put it bluntly, we have been raping our planet's resources for the last several hundred years. In our hearts, we know that this pattern of behaviour will have to stop before we can restore personal and global balance but we now have a deep fear of change because we are increasingly insulated from the natural cycles of death and rebirth, which are fundamental to the laws of nature.

Many people have recognised the wisdom in the myths that describe a champion's transformation and empowerment after facing adversity because there is a message of wholeness in the rich symbolism encoded in these kinds of tales. This often comes with an intuitive understanding that something of value remains hidden in these stories – an ancient knowledge that is sensed but difficult to define.

Genuine spiritual truths have a way of continuing to speak across time and culture but the language of symbol and metaphor needs to be transposed into the more linear concepts of the rational mind before we can fully comprehend the message and its relevance to the predicaments of our modern world. This need for understanding became the focus of my personal search for healing and meaning a number of years ago and I had a clear sense of looking for answers in the ancient traditions of the past.

In my search, I explored many myths and legends from a wide variety of sources. As I started to recover the core aspects of the forgotten secrets of the feminine principle, I realised that this knowledge contained information about the processes of creative manifestation and spiritual transformation as well. As I unravelled the layers of complex symbolism which are woven into so many myths, I began to see that some sources offered different aspects and perspectives of the same underlying theme and that others also contained fragments that hinted of a limitless source of potential creativity.

Each story seemed to be like a beautiful gem or bead, something complete in itself, but also a part of something bigger. Eventually, I stumbled upon a very old account of the archetypal inner journey of transformation. Miraculously, this source was uncorrupted and complete. With another cycle of research, cross-referencing and intuition, a consistent pattern finally crystallised as a jumble of interlaced threads organised itself, to reveal the underlying and unifying motif.

The complete design is composed of layers of pattern organised into a circular form because the mysteries of the feminine creative powers cannot be defined with the rational thought processes of the logical mind alone. They will continue to belong to the realm of the numinous, the potential of the undefined and the feeling of the sense of 'perhaps'. This will always be so because logic is only one aspect of human consciousness, even if it does try to rule the roost in a vain attempt to keep the rest of the psyche under its control.

I have called this reclaiming of ancient knowledge 'The Trail of the Black Madonna'. About 200 Black madonnas sit in Catholic churches all over Europe as tantalising reminders of the legacy of the Dark Goddess, the mysterious symbol of the transforming powers of the feminine principle. These statues encode the forgotten secrets of the circular dynamic between the eternal, creative polarities of the masculine and feminine energies as they are played out in human purpose to be mirrored back in the manifest world around us.

In many ancient cultures, the three aspects of the goddess, the feminine creative principle, were defined as the Virgin, the Mother and the Crone, and we can glean an understanding of their nature and powers from various myths and traditions. In ancient Greece and Rome, the qualities of love, beauty and fertility were associated with the goddess Venus and her counterpart, Aphrodite. Tradition has it that Aphrodite had a golden girdle, which was made for her by her husband, Hephaestus, the god of the alchemical arts of smith-craft. The story goes that, whenever Aphrodite wore her girdle, she became so sexually alluring that no man could resist her charms.

This is an encoded reference to the seemingly magical ability of the pure, virginal aspect of the feminine which has the power to magnetically pull or attract the electrical potential of the masculine principle towards itself. When the 'seed' of a new idea or concept is received into the matrix of the Virgin's womb, there is a conception, a new learning or beginning becomes possible and another twist of fate is initiated. The Virgin must learn how to make use of her power of discrimination as she magnetically selects a spark of male inspiration because she knows that she cannot give space to every new seed that comes looking for a home to grow in!

A Virgin with integrity and genuine purpose has to take a lot of care. It is very easy to get lost in the sentimentality of a pipe dream or forgotten in the illusion of someone else's chase. Venus had to learn how to use her powers of discernment and reject any unsuitable offers. It would have been a shameful waste of her valuable potential if she fell for the lure of a mate's empty pledge or prostituted her charm on the fickle, the stupid or the ridiculous.

Unfortunately, this aspect of the feminine power has become rather debased and undervalued, especially by women. It is a sacred quality, now often dismissed as the glamour of shallow allure or the superficial promise of empty sex, an act done in exchange for material security rather than genuine love. Paradoxically, the mysteriously attractive aspect of this quality is still sometimes recognised. Even political spin-doctors sense that they must 'sex up' their shifty policies in a vain attempt to make them appear more inviting to an increasingly suspicious electorate.

After incubation and gestation, the child of the new project is born but then it must be sustained and nurtured or it will come to nothing and die. This means that the second aspect of the feminine must come into play. These are the qualities of the Mother, who employs time, care and commitment to feed, nourish and maintain her new invention. Traditionally, this aspect of the feminine was symbolised as a gentle cow with her teats full of creamy milk, or by the cornucopia, a symbol of the endless supply of the fruits of the earth, a boundless resource of goodies that never becomes exhausted.

This aspect of the feminine principle is the one now most taken for granted, so it is here that we will find the deepest wounding, reflected in Mother Earth as well as in the individual and collective psyche. The Mother needs to be appreciated as she demonstrates her care by being there and providing for us. She is fulfilled in her service of feeding and caring but she also needs to be thanked, a respectful response which gives her something in return.

The Mother asks only that her children grow up to take charge of their own lives. Now, all too often, the pattern is one of greed, angry spoil and careless waste. This is followed by blame towards a Mother who has given out so much that she has actually become exhausted, unable to provide for anymore. As a last resort, the Mother can defend herself by learning how to withdraw. She cannot start all over again because her investment is already too great, but she can develop her powers of correction if she sees that her children have become irresponsible.

The Mother can learn how to withhold her nourishment by using her sacred right to say 'No' to abuse. In doing so, she risks that her domain will become a winter, but, in a wasteland of ruin and famine, her children will have the chance to see what they are doing and learn a new way of being. By withholding, the Mother hopes that her unconscious, destructive children will develop the awareness to come to their senses. To do this, she must face her fear of censure and honestly examine her motive.

True mother-love knows how to feign cruelty because it recognises the chance of engendering kindness in the recklessness of her offspring. When the Mother releases her fear that it is bad to appear to stop caring, she can let go of her children so that they can face the product of their excesses to learn their own responsibility, with no one but themselves to blame.

It is usually assumed that the Virgin and the Mother have it all but we have been fooled into disregarding the potential of the rest of life with the lie that we become barren or impotent in maturity. This is the third phase of creativity, the realm of the Dark Mother, or Crone. In maturity, there is another possibility; the chance to move beyond the sexual creativity of biology to initiate a higher power of transformation and move into the truth of a consciously creative and spiritual life.

When the Virgin Mother is willing to let go of her role of conceiving and caring for children, she has the chance of transforming herself as a third realm, the domain of sovereignty and limitless dark, opens up. By moving past anger and facing the demons of fear and incomprehension, another octave of creativity is presented. This potential was symbolised by the image of the Black Madonna, the three aspects of the Goddess, the feminine principle, integrated, fused together into one.

So, now you have guessed her secret – the Black Madonna is a symbol of a mother's care and a virgin's unconditional love but also of death, transformation and hence, rebirth. A ripple of shock moves through the reader... That's OK – but not for me! The forgotten secret is that she told us how we can change, creatively and lovingly. In spite of persecution, she managed to leave enough encoded instructions behind so we would know how to understand the processes of transformation and grow spiritually with compassion rather than fear. This reveals another of her secrets, the wisdom of the Underworld Initiation, an archetypal knowledge that actually explains the inner sequence of changes in the psyche that happen in all processes of growth and transformation.

There are many stories about this ancient tradition and we still sense their powerful mystery even though some of the details have become rather fragmented as misunderstandings crept in over time. These are the myths that we intuitively label 'archetypal', ready to leave it at that. But why are they archetypal? Why do they resonate so deeply and what exactly are they trying to say?

These stories explain something deep and complex because the transformation of consciousness at the heart of every spiritual tradition is impossible to put into a linear framework of words based purely on logic. This is why I could not uncover this information with logic alone and why this book looks at three stories, each one an apparently different version of the same thing.

Each myth presents a different slant or focus, so together they offer more than the sum of their parts. When they are threaded like beads making a necklace, the thread links them together and they become something more, the sort of alchemy of consciousness that is always at the source of the power of the Black Madonna. As you link the stories together in your mind, there will be glimpses of her hidden qualities. When the mind has a more conscious understanding of the intuitive processes that are inherent in the transformation of change, it is much more likely to relax enough to allow a feeling, a feeling that offers the gift of alchemy in the heart.

I. Threading the Beads of Myth and Symbol

IT IS ESTIMATED THAT ABOUT 200 CHURCHES IN EUROPE contain unusual statues of the Madonna and her Child, purposefully created with very dark or black skin. These representations occur in a large area, in churches across France, Belgium, Germany, Spain, Portugal, Italy and Poland. Some are carved from wood and others from stone. If the wood or stone was not naturally dark in colour, the faces and hands have been stained so that they become dark, often in a striking contrast to the eyes and teeth which are white.

From their condition and style, it is clear that most of these madonnas are very old. Local records show that some date from the 11th and 12th centuries;[1] others are known to be copies of even earlier originals. One at La Deliverande, in the Calvados region of France, is a copy of a 4th-century stone statue unearthed by grazing sheep in the 11th century but subsequently destroyed. A surprising number were found buried in the ground or purposefully hidden. One, made of black stone, in

---

[1] 'Black Madonnas in France', www.udayton.edu.

I. Threading the Beads of Myth and Symbol

the church at Sarrance in the Pyrenees, was unearthed in the 8th century by a bull; another, at Gerzat, was found by shepherds, hidden in rocks by a spring. Several were discovered in the 11th and 12th centuries, carefully preserved in hollow trees or logs found buried in the ground.

Why were so many of these madonnas hidden, to be found in curious circumstances centuries later? The most likely answer is because there was persecution by the growing power of the Christian church, especially during the Middle Ages and the Reformation. It is known that a number of the black madonnas are copies that were made to replace older versions, which were destroyed by the Huguenots in the 15th century.

Together, these facts suggest that the black madonnas are a legacy of an earlier spiritual tradition, a legacy that the Church was at pains to suppress. It has been suggested that there is a link with the French legend that Mary Magdalene came to France from the Holy Land after the Crucifixion, a speculation made more likely by the concentration of black madonnas in the area of the Languedoc in France. The story is that Mary Magdalene arrived by boat with Mary, the Mother of Jesus, and another woman, Sara – their black, Egyptian servant – at a place now known as Les Saintes-Maries de la Mer (the Saint Marys of the Sea), on the Mediterranean coast of southern France.

While I am sure that this is one aspect of the truth of the black madonnas, I think that there is another link to be explored, a link which leads back to Isis, the most important goddess in ancient Egypt. As the mother of the child god, Horus, Isis is the key figure in the myth of Osiris and Seth and there are a number of ancient Egyptian paintings and statues of Isis that show her seated on a throne with her son, Horus, on her lap, showing an uncanny resemblance to the style and form of some of the older black madonnas in France.

When Alexander the Great conquered Egypt in 332 BCE, the first historical links between the civilisations and traditions of Greece and Egypt were born. Alexander built his famous library in the delta of the River Nile[2] and created one of the seven wonders of the ancient world. This became one of the most important centres of teaching as many people travelled across the Mediterranean Sea to learn and share information. It was here that the Greek, Archimedes, invented the first screw-shaped water pump and Euclid discovered the rules of geometry. For nearly 300 years, the brightest minds met together as the ancient mysteries of the gods of the Pharaohs fertilised the Greek aptitude for invention and applied logic.

Later, in 48 BCE, Julius Caesar brought his Roman army into Egypt. Caesar famously had an affair with the Egyptian queen, Cleopatra, and in her bid for a political alliance, the cross-fertilisation between these two cultures was cemented for ever. Following their leader, Roman soldiers must have imbibed something of Egypt's mysteries as they embraced their lovers, all

---

[2] 'Library of Alexandria Discovered' by Dr David Whitehouse, www.news.bbc.co.uk

followers of Isis. Later, because the Roman desire to conquer was relentless, some of these Egyptian secrets would have found their way into the heart of the Roman army as it marched its way across Europe. Two thousand years later in Britain, the upper reaches of the River Thames at Oxford are still known locally as the River Isis, a name unfamiliar in the English language and not obviously related to any other local gods and goddesses.

So it is quite possible that Isis became well known in Europe, carried on the back of the Roman army and probably merging with the goddesses of the existing local traditions. But why are the 'Isis' madonnas portrayed with dark skin? The Egyptian civilisation did extend down into Nubia, and from 760–653 BCE, Egypt was ruled by a dynasty of black Nubians,[3] so this is one explanation, but there is also another one.

In many ancient traditions, the feminine principle was described as having three aspects or forms, each one having a different set of qualities, powers or attributes. These aspects were represented by various goddesses in different cultures but sometimes there was a kind of 'chief' goddess, one who had the ability to encompass all three aspects within the one form, Isis being a classic example.

The three aspects of the goddess were usually symbolised as the Virgin, the Mother and the Wise Woman or Crone, each one having a colour symbolising their

---

[3] 'Nubian Rulers of Egypt', www.homestead.com.

particular power. White was associated with the Virgin aspect as a symbol of purity and innocence; red was connected with the Mother as a symbol of the blood of menstruation, childbirth and the maternal bloodline. Black was the colour of the Dark Goddess, the Crone, mistress of the Underworld cycles of change, death and rebirth, together with the mysteries of spiritual transformation. If an artist wanted to portray the three aspects of the feminine in one statue, then what better way than to show a mother holding her child (the Mother and the Virgin) and then make them black to signify that the mother also embodied the Dark Goddess, the Crone?

In the archetypal story of Isis, Osiris and Horus, Isis actively demonstrates her command of the three aspects of the feminine powers in the various twists and turns of the plot but there is an emphasis of her magical knowledge of the mysteries of the Dark Goddess. The Crone rules the powers of the 'dark', the transforming realms of spiritual rebirth that make up the Underworld regions of the deep earth. She is the feared Kali of the Hindus, the awesome Gorgon Medusa of the Greeks and the apparently cruel Ereshkigal from Sumer. Her power is the tough love of authenticity and a truth based on unsentimental integrity, an almost forgotten power that has the ability to make or break, an inner strength carved by surviving the tests of adversity.

I believe that we have been denied the wisdom of the Dark Mother for far too long, that we have errone-

I. Threading the Beads of Myth and Symbol

ously been taught to fear her and that we all need her inspiration now, more than ever. Her teachings embody the true power of the feminine, the eternal 'She' who has the power to face the Underworld of unconscious denial and navigate the confusion of abuse so that she can retrieve the essence of unconditional love that lies at the core of her being. I became determined to find her as I followed her trail back through centuries of distortion, looking for the fragments of half-forgotten teachings, convinced that her message was still there, hidden in the mysteries of the past.

Finally she revealed herself and then I started to realise that she had been there all along but that I had not understood what I was looking for. Suddenly I could see her influence everywhere as it traced through a hundred stories, the so-called fairy tales and myths that we have been told were nonsense or fantasy. She had been there all the time, peeping from paintings and carvings, hiding behind symbols and colours. When she shared some of her secrets, I knew that it was on one condition: that I was willing to share them too.

This knowledge was known in the past but it works just as well today as it ever did because the nature of human consciousness has not changed that much in the last several thousand years. This information used to be an intrinsic part of everyday living, available to everyone when they were ready to receive it. Admittedly, some of the deeper aspects were guarded more carefully but this was only because they could be damaging if the psyche of the person was not yet ready to inte-

I. Threading the Beads of Myth and Symbol

grate them. The essence of this wisdom became the stuff of symbol and myth, handed down primarily in an oral tradition, the legacy of which still surrounds us today.

As I attempted to write about this forgotten knowledge as rationally as possible, I realised that it defied a linear approach and I have therefore had to surrender to that. My original training in science reared its head a number of times and I dutifully made chapter lists and rationales, but as the title suggests, the underlying theme is circular because a purely linear approach just won't do.

The premise is that there is a common or underlying spiritual truth hidden in many, if not all, ancient symbols and traditions. This is not a new idea and lots of people have already carefully collated the hundreds of myths and legends of many countries so that their similarities and themes can become clearly apparent. I could not have done what I have done without all of this thorough research and I am grateful that so many have spent so much time gathering information in this way.

With all of these stories swirling at my fingertips, something else was added to the brew and eventually, the scattered parts of a complex jigsaw puzzle started to order themselves as an underlying pattern finally emerged. That 'something else' could be called intuition, a simple word for one of those illusive mysteries of life, and I'll leave it at that for now!

I have attempted to make each section more or less complete in itself, so, like beads that are a part of a

I. Threading the Beads of Myth and Symbol

necklace, they can be looked at together or examined one by one on their own. Inside each bead there is a connecting thread linking them all together. The thread is the teaching of the Underworld Initiation and the method of the transformation in spiritual consciousness which lies at the heart of this ancient ritual.

Human consciousness is very complex because it functions on many levels at once. Words and speech use the rational aspect of the mind but this can be compared with the tip of an iceberg as most of our awareness continues to function, largely undetected, out of airy sight, in the watery seas of the unconscious. The Underworld Initiation was designed to teach the navigation of these Elemental seas of consciousness but this is not a logical journey and another set of directions comes into play as soon as you put your head under the water. It can take a while to get your sea legs and seasickness is not uncommon, but the rewards are great and there is real treasure hidden at the bottom of the ocean after the monsters of the deep have been tamed.

II. The Story of Isis, Osiris and Horus
The Mysteries of Rebirth and Resurrection

THE ORIGINS OF THE STORY OF ISIS BRINGING HER husband's spirit back to life so that she could magically conceive her son, are lost to the mists of time. This is an archetypal story in every sense of the word and it has many levels of meaning and interpretation. In my adaptation and commentary, I am going to focus on the aspects that I feel are relevant to the mysteries of the Underworld Initiation, so that themes, symbols and metaphors that relate to this ancient tradition can be revealed.

As one of the oldest of myths, many versions evolved during the course of Egypt's long history.[4] This tale became a kind of foundation stone for the whole of the Egyptian religion because it links the god, Osiris, with the cycles of death and rebirth in the Underworld realms and, through his son, Horus, there was a link with the cycle of succession through which a new Pharaoh could become the next king. As the wife of

---

[4] *The Legend of Osiris*, by David C Scott, www.touregypt.net/godsofegypt.

II. The Secret of Isis, Osiris and Horus

Osiris and the mother of Horus, Isis has a central role in the story as she moves between the realms of the mysteries of the Goddess, demonstrating the various powers of the feminine principle.

As an ancient archetype of the feminine powers of creativity, Isis was known in Egypt as the Goddess of Ten Thousand Names and she has a counterpart in every tradition. One of the hieroglyphs associated with her was called the Knot or Girdle of Isis, which variously translates as 'life', 'welfare' or the 'blood' of Isis. It takes the form of a long sash or girdle with the two ends knotted or buckled together. In this form, the Knot of Isis was often carved from carnelian, jasper or red glass and hung around the neck of an embalmed mummy as a magical amulet of protection that would ward off evil spirits as the soul returned to the Underworld. When it was paired with another hieroglyph, the 'djed pillar', the symbol of her husband, Osiris, these two hieroglyphs alluded to one of the threads of the Underworld mysteries, the secrets of the dynamic between the eternal energies of the feminine and masculine principles as they are played out in the creativity of human purpose, mirrored back in the manifest world around us.

In the legend, Osiris and Isis rule Egypt as the first Pharaoh and his Queen. As the great-grandson of the mighty Ra, Osiris was well known as a fair and just ruler. With his Queen, they created a kind of Golden Age, a time of peace and plenty when all the sacred laws of Ma'at were observed and honoured.

II. The Secret of Isis, Osiris and Horus

Osiris had a brother, Seth. In time, Seth became jealous of Osiris. He wanted the power of the throne of Egypt for himself and he coveted Isis, the beautiful Queen. Eventually, Seth thought of a plot to kill his brother so he could take the throne and rule the people of Egypt. Seth had a devious mind and he knew that he would have to use the black arts to trick Osiris. He built a wooden box like a coffin with a lid and marked it with magical, binding spells that would trap whoever went inside it. Once inside, no one would be able to escape because they would be magically chained inside the box for ever.

On the next feast day of the gods, Seth took the wooden box to the palace. He waited for the end of the evening's celebrations, when even Osiris was drunk, and then he challenged Osiris to a contest of strength. Seth placed the box in front of Osiris saying that they would each take a turn to get inside and then try to force the lid off with their physical strength alone. Osiris wasn't thinking straight so he agreed to get in first. As soon as Osiris got inside, Seth leapt forward and closed the lid, sealing the top tight with molten lead. Osiris fought with all his might but the spells of black magic held him down, and because the box was sealed, he eventually died. Seth took the box and threw it into the River Nile, letting it float away.

Seth took over the throne of Egypt and tried to make Isis his Queen. Everyone was afraid of him because they knew that he had the power of black magic as well as his physical force. It was a dark time for Egypt. Seth

II. The Secret of Isis, Osiris and Horus

was cruel and he had no understanding of the divine laws of Ma'at which usually kept the peace and fertility of the kingdom. Before long, war divided the great lands of Egypt as the people fought with one another.

Isis was the only one who would not give in to Seth. She was not afraid of his evil ways and she was determined to recover the body of her husband in the hope that she might be able to revive him. She went down to the Nile where she searched its banks for the wooden box. Finally she found it, on the side of the Nile, at Byblos. After floating down the Nile, the wooden box had become lodged in a tamarisk bush. This had grown into a huge tree because of the strong spirit of Osiris still inside the box nearby.

In some versions of the story, it is said that the huge trunk of the tamarisk tree had grown to completely envelope the box. When the tree was felled, its trunk had been taken to make a column to hold up the roof of the palace of the King of Phoenicia. Isis had to go to the King's palace in disguise and then use her magic wand to summon up thunder and lightning to split the huge log apart and recover the box inside.[5] It is thought that the hieroglyph for Osiris, djed, 'the backbone of Osiris', represents the trunk of the tree that grew so strongly around his coffin.

When Isis tore off the lid of the box, she found Osiris lifeless inside. She wept as she realised that she was too late but she was determined to give Osiris a proper

---

[5] *Ancient Egyptian Magic*, by Cassandra Eason, published by Vega, 2003.

II. The Secret of Isis, Osiris and Horus

funeral, so, in mourning, she carried the coffin back to Egypt and placed it in the House of the Gods. Isis then went to find the god Thoth, because she thought it might be possible to bring Osiris back to life and she knew that Thoth would be able to help her. Thoth was the Egyptian god of wisdom, writing and the spoken word. It was said that he brought creation into existence because he had the power to voice the thoughts of the Creator out loud. He was also the god of healing, medicine and magical knowledge, so if anyone could help, it would be Thoth.

While Isis was away, the evil Seth went to the House of the Gods and stole Osiris's body. To make sure that Isis had no chance to work her magic, Seth cut the corpse into fourteen pieces, which he scattered throughout the length and breadth of Egypt. Seth thought that if Osiris's corpse was in pieces, then his spirit would not be able to return to it and then there would be no possibility that he could be resurrected.

Isis refused to be put off. With the help of her sister, Nephthys, and the frog goddess, Heket, she searched all of Egypt until she found the scattered pieces of Osiris's body. Eventually she found them all except his phallus. Nephthys, Isis and Heket gathered the pieces of Osiris and took them first to Thoth, so that Thoth could work his magic on them. Thoth then took the pieces to Anubis, the black jackal-headed god of the Underworld.

Anubis created the first mummy from the fourteen parts of Osiris's body. He carefully washed all the pieces

II. The Secret of Isis, Osiris and Horus

so that, after stitching them back together, he could embalm the body and wrap it round with lengths of linen. Isis made a phallus to replace the one which they could not find and then, together with Thoth, she cast the ritual of life, which allows us all to live for ever. This included the ceremony of the opening of the mouth so the spirit of Osiris could enter into his body again.

Isis then changed herself into a bird. In the form of a sparrow hawk, she swooped around the body of Osiris, singing the magical words that Thoth had taught her. As the breath of life stirred again in Osiris, Isis could receive his spirit into her body to be impregnated and conceive a child. In this way, Isis became pregnant with the child of Osiris, a boy who she named Horus, the hawk.

After this, Osiris went to live in the Underworld because he could not stay in the land of the living. Anubis gave up his throne so that Osiris could become the lord of the dead. Together they passed judgement on the souls who passed through the Underworld. Isis went to the dense marshes of papyrus on the delta of the Nile to hide from Seth. She knew that Seth would try to kill her son so she had to give birth alone and hide until Horus came of age.

Seth was furious when he heard that Isis had managed to conceive a son by Osiris but eventually he calmed down when he realised that even the magic of Isis and Thoth could not bring Osiris back to the realm of the land of the living. Seth came to believe that he

II. The Secret of Isis, Osiris and Horus

would be able to sit on the throne of Egypt for all time.

Hidden on the island in the delta of the Nile, Horus grew to be a strong boy and even though Seth sent serpents and demons to kill him, Horus always defeated them. Horus was determined to challenge his evil uncle, so when he came of age, Isis taught him her magic and Thoth gave him a knife to fight with.

Seth and Horus fought each other for many days but in the end, Seth was defeated and Horus castrated him with the knife. Horus cast Seth into the darkness, where he still lives, constantly seeking revenge. It is prophesied that one day Horus and Seth will fight again for control of the world but Horus, this time, will defeat Seth for ever. This means that Osiris will be able to return on the Day of Awakening. When all the tombs are opened, those who lived a just life will live again as all sorrow passes away for ever.

III. The Teachings of Isis, a Black Madonna

MOST ENDURING LEGENDS HAVE SEVERAL LAYERS OF meaning that interweave through the tale, giving them the capacity to speak symbolically to many people at different stages of their life journey. This myth is particularly complex because each of the main characters acts out a number of roles at once as they convey their multilevel messages. With this in mind, I'll concentrate on picking out some of the themes as they relate to the Black Madonna and the eternal cycles of death and rebirth because these are important parts of the Underworld tradition.

Isis has a central role and she reveals the various powers of the feminine principle as the story's events unfold. She has the ability to move between all the aspects of the divine feminine, demonstrating the magical power of the 'virginal' conception as well as the practical, resourceful and nurturing characteristics of the mother raising and protecting her child on her own. She also facilitates Osiris's 'magical' rebirth and transformation, with the powers of the 'Dark Mother' she can creatively fuse all the feminine qualities

III. The Teachings of Isis, a Black Madonna

together. Isis is willing to ask for help and she refuses to give up in the face of adversity, intuitively sensing that there is always another answer if the first one fails. The feminine approach is to look for the bigger picture, knowing that the overview and the long view are more likely to give the most enduring or beneficial results.

The ancient tradition of the four primordial powers of creative manifestation, often called the four Elements, also subtly interweaves through the various events. This concept was one of the foundation stones of most ancient traditions, the idea being that there are a number of primary forces or qualities that function together as a kind of energetic 'pre-matter', which colours or influences the processes that precipitate matter into form.

In the West, we are more familiar with this concept in terms of the four Elements, but some cultures concentrate on three and others use five. In the ancient Greek tradition, these powers were known as earth, water, fire and air. In the Native American tradition they are known as the four directions – north, south, east and west – and in the Welsh Bardic tradition of the Celts, they were known as the Anadyl, the four sacred breaths, winds or *pneuma*, that animate all of life. In the Christian tradition they became synonymous with the four archangels and in Europe, the mediaeval alchemists worked with the concept of the four humours, qualities that related emotional characteristics with aspects of the physical body. In this way the four Elements were understood to have an influence on the health of the

III. The Teachings of Isis, a Black Madonna

individual. They are also an important aspect of astrology, a tradition that was certainly known to the ancient Egyptians.

The symbolism of the four Elements appears in the story in various ways, a number of times. The most obvious expression of the water Element are the references to the River Nile but it also appears as the tears of mourning that Isis sheds when she finds the lifeless body of Osiris. The earth Element is suggested when the box containing Osiris is washed up out of the Nile and onto the river bank, a sort of enactment of the primordial act of Creation in many early myths which describes the first mound of land rising up from the sea. Another aspect of the earth Element is the reference to Seth dismembering the body of Osiris into fourteen pieces, the physical body being the earthy aspect of human experience. Isis summons the fire Element to release Osiris from his entombment inside the trunk of the tamarisk tree and air is expressed in the magical words that Thoth teaches Isis so that she can sing the spirit of Osiris back to his mummified body.

In some ways, Thoth acts as a kind of personification of the air Element. He knows how to speak the sacred word, a power that he passes on to Isis. Later in the story, Thoth gives Horus the gift of a magical knife to help him in his battle with Seth. The magical knife or sword appears in many ancient myths as the symbol of the power of the air Element with its ability to summon insight, to cut through deception, to see through illusion and hence bring spiritual clarity to a situation.

III. The Teachings of Isis, a Black Madonna

As the archetypal trickster in the story, Seth actively demonstrates the negative expression of this Element's power when he uses his devious mind and slippery tongue to trick Osiris with spells of black magic and evil intent. Airy fairy air can seem innocent enough but it has a hidden command over the other three Elemental powers, something which exponents of its negative arts exploit because they know that it is difficult to spot.

In my understanding, the qualities of the four Elements are one of the most important, forgotten secrets of the Underworld tradition. Once their symbolism is understood, it becomes obvious that they appear in some form or another in many myths, acting as the mysterious 'X' factors that link the physical manifestation of events in the outer world with the subjective changes in consciousness which are a part of the inner worlds of the learning experience within the psyche. It is more or less impossible to explain how these powers operate by using the rational linearity of the ordinary, day-to-day mental aspects of the human mind alone because this logical aspect of human consciousness 'cannot get its head around it', literally.

The energetic qualities of the four Elements operate through a numinous sense of feeling–perception that is highly subjective and extremely mysterious to the rational mind but they are an absolutely vital aspect of human consciousness, something which the Underworld tradition of every culture I have looked at was trying to explain. To me, they are an answer to the

III. The Teachings of Isis, a Black Madonna

Alchemical riddle of 'as above, so below' as well as being linked with other mysterious, ancient terms such as the 'lost chord', the 'food of life' and the 'water of life', to name but a few.

When Isis used her mysterious powers of incantation, she was summoning the four Elements because she needed this 'magic' to call the spirit of Osiris back to his body. Isis also uses this kind of power when she calls for fire, in the form of thunder and lightning, so that she can split open the tamarisk column and retrieve the precious box hidden inside.

Part of the reason why we have turned away from this knowledge is because these powers can be consciously used in negative ways, an evil trait or 'sin', which the character, Seth, clearly exhibits. The trouble is that we are all using these powers, largely unconsciously, all day, every day, in everything that we think and do, sometimes hurting ourselves and others without knowing what we are doing and how we are doing it. This clarifies another important hidden message from Isis: the understanding that it is possible to learn how to become conscious of how we are using the powers of the four Elements so that we can transform negative and destructive patterns of behaviour into their positive, creative counterparts, using love as a motive instead of anger and fear.

If we understand the ways in which these powers can be used in all their positive and negative manifestations, it then becomes obvious when another person is using them against us because we can see what they

III. The Teachings of Isis, a Black Madonna

are up to and how they are doing it. This means that we don't have to 'buy into' negative patterns of behaviour anymore, no longer needing to play the victim of an abuse or misuse of power. In the terms of the story, Seth's negative spells or energy workings are reversed so that Elemental power can be used in positive ways for the benefit of all. In the story, this understanding is symbolised when Horus grows up. When he is old enough, he can use Thoth's knife of insight together with the 'magic' given to him by Isis, to do battle with Seth and defeat him.

This shift from a fearful, negative expression to a conscious, loving, positive use of Elemental power, is the essential change in consciousness that lies at the heart of the Underworld Initiation itself. The Underworld's 'Day of Judgement' refers to the ability of the soul's aspect of our awareness to assess the outcome of the life path or journey and to see whether we have understood our 'Elementary' lessons in attending our classes in earth school experience. If we have got the point and have ticked all the boxes in the correct sequence, then that lifetime will be complete even though we may have to come back again to have a go at a 'diploma course', another set of lessons in another lifetime.

More and more people are having this kind of look at the overview of their life in near-death experiences or other, similar circumstances. Sometimes a choice is possible on the karmic level and the soul might decide to return to the physical body and continue to live for

III. The Teachings of Isis, a Black Madonna

further opportunities for spiritual growth. In other cases, the planned lifetime's experiences might be complete, in which case the person will 'die' as they move on to the non-physical levels of being and leave their physical body behind. In other karmic situations, there is a choice and the soul may chose to carry on in the physical dimension, their spirit returning to their body for another series of learning situations, perhaps continuing to support other members of their soul group who still need to be 'physical'.

If we are very keen to get our spiritual lessons done, there may be the chance of 'going for broke' by attempting to reach for 'the big apple', the possibility of seeing through the game of life whilst still alive on the physical level. This understanding relates to realising that the most essential life task is to focus on the process of becoming more and more conscious of how we are creating what happens to us every day with as much love and responsibility as we can muster from moment to moment. It then becomes possible to break through or transform spiritual consciousness or life perspective, another aspect of the encoded meaning of the word 'rebirth' in the Underworld stories and, incidentally, the hidden message behind the story of Eve offering an apple to Adam.

When we have learned how to use the various powers of the four Elements in their positive, loving expressions, an inner state of harmony and balance becomes possible, something which the Egyptians referred to as living in accordance with the laws of

Ma'at, cosmic or divine justice. The Gnostics called this 'Sophia', another description of the higher perspective of the pure, 'virginal', cosmic resonance of the feminine principle fused with a comprehension of the cycles and rhythms of Mother Earth, the wisdom of the 'Dark Mother'. Horus, as the child of rebirth born from the womb of the Dark Mother, becomes the physical expression of the inner transformation and Elemental alchemy of the psyche, the product of the change in awareness which has released negative, fearful patterns of behaviour to reveal new levels of looking at things, motivated by unconditional love and the highest good of all.

IV. The Mystery of the Underworld Initiation

FOR A LONG TIME I HAD SENSED THAT THERE WAS AN underlying set of core teachings that was the foundation of all ancient wisdom and eventually my research led me to recover the sequence of the Underworld Initiation. This was a spiritual ritual known to many ancient cultures but, because it was labelled pagan or heretical and persecuted by the Christian Church, much of the information about it became hidden or highly obscured.

My first source for these teachings was the Sumerian myth of Inanna because it includes, in great detail, the story of Inanna's journey into the 'Great Below', the Underworld itself. With this information, I was able to go back to the Egyptian myth of Isis and Osiris and glean another layer of understanding from this version of the same process of initiation. Later, I looked at Chrétien's myth of Perceval's quest for the Holy Grail, and realised that I was seeing another version of the same archetypal story, perhaps more accessible to us because it was written not so very long ago. Eventually, by comparing the symbolism and the themes from the various versions

IV. The Mystery of the Underworld Initiation

of the Underworld Initiation, I managed to piece the fragments together and a consistent pattern emerged.

In the past, the Underworld Initiation, in its various forms, was a ritual designed to give the candidate a direct, conscious experience of the mysteries of the Dark Goddess. This process of initiation was undertaken by both men and women with the purpose of provoking a dramatic shift in consciousness which would result in a greater understanding of the life purpose as well as a direct spiritual experience of the inner consciousness of the soul, usually sensed or symbolised in female form. This shift in awareness has a profound effect on the rest of the psyche and this was the real purpose of the ritual.

In many ancient cultures it was understood that in the normal processes of growing up, the soul's focus of consciousness would become forgotten or hidden in the Underworld, what we would now call the unconscious mind. In a sense, this has to happen. The innocent, eternal, spiritual perspective of the soul is the primary focus of our awareness as children but it has to retreat into the background as the ego-mind begins to develop. The soul is not lost but it becomes forgotten. It metaphorically sinks into the deep 'seas' of the unconscious mind where it remains as a rather mysterious and elusive hidden source of spiritual and intuitive guidance. The soul becomes the inner siren of our dreams, occasionally emerging into consciousness unexpectedly, perhaps in the euphoria of falling in love or as an inner voice that tells us what to do in a time of physical danger.

IV. The Mystery of the Underworld Initiation

In childhood, we are taught to focus our 'outer' attention on learning the numerous skills that we need to function as social human beings. In this process, we gradually develop an internal, but outwardly facing, energetic structure aspect of the conscious mind which Freud first defined as 'the ego'. This mechanism of the mind was understood in ancient Greece when they used masks to portray the personas of the various characters in their celebrated plays. The ego ends up behaving just like a mask as it gradually develops in childhood and adolescence as a kind of complex screen or energy shield through which we learn to interact with the world and those around us.

The energy structure that makes up the ego is a completely necessary aspect of human awareness. It is the mental mechanism for integrating new learning experiences because it has the power to combine rational thought, memory, physical sensation and emotional feeling. It gives us the ability to think something through, and to compare and contrast. With it we can gather information, plan an action, learn how to do something and then judge the outcome. In many ways, it is the biological equivalent of the most highly complex on-board computer that could ever be imagined.

So what's wrong with that? Nothing, except that as we get older, the ego has a tendency, like every computer, to get stuck in habits and routines, and because it looks outward, it forgets why it does the things that it does. It usually gets narrow-minded, controlling, manipulative and entrenched as it gets lost in old

IV. The Mystery of the Underworld Initiation

unconscious, negative belief systems that make it fearful of change and potential loss. From the soul's point of view, when this starts to happen, these negative ego characteristics become something of a limitation or liability because new information is stopped from coming in. When the ego becomes too entrenched or controlling, it won't embrace the expanded vision of the spiritual perspective because it has become resistant to further growth.

Something has to give and this was the point of the Underworld Initiation. The ritual was designed to test and shock. It had to be rigorous and slightly threatening so that the negative, dominating aspects of the ego's energetic structures could be broken apart and shattered. In today's terms we might call this a mental or emotional breakdown. In the myth of Isis and Osiris, this breakdown is symbolised when the evil Seth cuts Osiris's (ego) body into fourteen pieces and scatters them throughout Egypt.

This process of shattering is painful but there is a deeper purpose behind it and in many ancient cultures, this was understood. The initiate knew that they would have to face and pass through the many layers of fear that normally lie hidden in the unconscious part of the mind, so that these fears, often symbolically portrayed as dragons or monsters, could be conquered and then transformed.

It was known that the unconscious mind also held many levels of ancestral or inherited fear as well as those created from personal experience. It was also

IV. The Mystery of the Underworld Initiation

known that the experience of moving through them would be harrowing. In the Sumerian version of the ritual, Inanna has to strip naked by taking layers of her clothing off, one by one, on her way down into the Underworld, this being symbolic of her ego structures being gradually dismantled. This means that she has no way of defending herself when she encounters Ereshkigal's terrifying onslaught. Ereshkigal has the role of the Dark Goddess as she 'attacks' the last aspects of Inanna's ego, and Inanna apparently dies as her 'corpse' is hung on a hook, like meat, to rot.

In the Greek myth of Theseus and the Minotaur, Theseus has to make his way to the centre of a labyrinth, a symbol of the convoluted twists and turns of the non-linear pathways of the unconscious mind. He must find and kill the Minotaur, a half man, half bull monster, that lives in the subterranean depths of the labyrinth, a particularly vivid portrayal of the fearful, primal emotions of the negative ego. In this case, the initiate, Theseus, is guided through the confusions of his inner journey by Ariadne's golden thread, a beautiful portrayal of the help and spiritual support of his hidden soul.

Isis could be understood as the soul aspect of her husband's psyche, the higher perception who has the guiding overview, recovering the broken pieces of his shattered ego before she draws his spirit back to his body. Her love is the power to revive him and with the help of Thoth's new spiritual insight, Isis can breathe new understanding and wisdom into a life which has been broken apart.

IV. The Mystery of the Underworld Initiation

After the process of ego breakdown there is a rebirth or spiritual renewal. Inanna is revived when she is given the magical gifts of the water of life and the food of life. Osiris's change in consciousness is symbolised by the birth of his child, Horus, conceived magically by Isis. Later, when Horus has grown up, he fights with his father's killer and manages to defeat him, a symbol of a new consciousness that has killed the demons of the past to become stronger and more balanced than before.

5. The Forgotten Knowledge of the Four Elements

THE FOUR ELEMENTS – EARTH, WATER, FIRE AND AIR – were understood to be the powers or principles that formed the basis or foundation of many different philosophies and spiritual traditions. These powers were held to be the fundamental forces, energies or powers of nature, each having specific qualities and functions. From the writings of the ancient Greeks, we can understand that these archetypal energies were viewed as vital qualities which combined together to form the physical matter of creation.

These four powers are still acknowledged in many world religions as well as most of the various Shamanic and native traditions. In the West, we are more familiar with the term 'the four Elements', because this comes from the writings of the ancient Greeks, but it does not matter if they are called angels, gods, the four winds or the four directions, both the principle and the understanding are the same.

These primordial powers can be seen as the energetic building blocks of existence. In combination, they are the colouring forces or qualities that lie behind the

V. The Forgotten Knowledge of the four Elements

make-up and manifestation of the substance of physical matter itself. Atomic physicists could one day realise that they have already witnessed the subatomic proof of the Elements of earth and fire that they have called quarks and leptons. In the cosmic 'glue' of existence, water's magnetic Elemental force field of love is an actuality, a fact that every person with healing hands already knows. One day they might be able to prove that the power of thought really does have the capacity to move things and the Element of air will have acknowledgement as the power of the idea, a concept that embodies a spark of spiritual energy, which may result in a physical manifestation.

So why did the significance of the four Elements get half lost and almost forgotten in Europe? There are two interrelated reasons. In the Middle Ages the growing influence of the Christian Church began to instigate a sustained and persistent persecution of the 'old ways', also known as the Celtic tradition, which the Church began to call pagan, heretic or heathen.

These terms were originally coined by the Church to describe those people who had not become a part of Christian religion but they developed into terms of censure and abuse. The word pagan comes from *'pagus'*, a Latin word meaning 'a rural district'.[6] When Christianity became the state religion in the Roman Empire, the people in the towns and cities were the first to convert while the country dwellers were more

---

[6] www.etymonline.com.

reluctant to change, staying with the old gods and goddesses for longer. The word 'heresy' comes from an old French word 'hérésie', this coming in turn from the Latin '*haeresis*', meaning a school of thought or a philosophical sect. Originally, it just meant 'having an opinion that was different from that of the Orthodox Church'.[7]

The real meaning of the four Elements became very fragmented over the centuries as many followers of the old ways were killed and thousands of ancient manuscripts were burnt, destroyed or secretly hidden. Also, the teachings of the pre-Christian religions were largely based on an oral tradition which was passed down directly from one person to another through ritual, verse, myth and symbol, so when thousands of so-called witches and heretics were killed by a Church trying to stamp out their legacy, there were few left to pass on their teachings.

There was a resurgence of this wisdom in the Renaissance, especially in the writings of the alchemists, but, by this time, because they were working in a climate of active persecution, their manuscripts had to be purposefully encrypted. This has made their understandings almost impossible to decipher although the power of their message still rings true. When the original, authentic sequence of the Underworld Initiation is understood, the alchemical language suddenly makes sense and the essence of their teachings becomes clear.

---

[7] www.etymonline.com.

V. The Forgotten Knowledge of the four Elements

From the legends and stories that have survived,[8] we know that the pre-Christian teachings of the Celts in Europe also stressed the importance of the immortal soul, the aspect of human consciousness that repeatedly reincarnates in the cyclical processes of physical death and rebirth. This is a powerful understanding when it is considered from the point of view of the individual soul. It means that each lifetime can be valued as a further opportunity for soul development and growth because it is understood that there is a spiritual purpose to each incarnation and that this is made up of various tests or karmic lessons.

The Celts also had the knowledge that every person is a member of a soul family or group so when someone died, they became one of the ancestors, souls on the non-physical levels of human existence who were still able to communicate spiritually with those who remained incarnate. The ancestors were able to guide and reassure those still living until it was time, in due course, for them to reincarnate and return to a physical form.

The combination of the knowledge that everyone has a soul that reincarnates plus the understanding of the importance of the four Elements as the agents of learning and empowerment along the life path, is an extremely powerful spiritual teaching. This information gradually leads to a growing sense of personal, inner, spiritual authority which empowers the individual to

---

[8] *Druidry – Rekindling the Sacred Art*, published by the British Druid Order, 1999.

V. The Forgotten Knowledge of the four Elements

take more and more loving responsibility for their own life. It also means that there is less possibility of the individual being controlled by those trying to usurp spiritual authority and power. With these understandings, a person cannot be controlled on a false moral or pseudo-spiritual level and the individual keeps responsibility for the unique process of the unfolding of their own unique path of spiritual development. This was probably the real reason why this ancient information became an anathema to the growing power base of the Church.

As an example, the essence of this issue became the spiritual struggle for power which lies behind the enduring myth of King Arthur. He became a symbol of the inner conflict and the outer battle of spiritual wills which the people were starting to experience in the Britain of the 6th and 7th centuries as the Church sought increasing spiritual and material authority.

We may never know the true identity of the man who gave his life fighting because of this dilemma, but I believe that his myth endures because we are still living with the ramifications of this conflict between personal morality and 'corporate' spiritual interests. In his story, we recognise our own dilemma as we continue to deal with the historical legacy which still deeply permeates the attitudes of our culture today.

As the Church grew in power and influence, it began its acts of persecution in earnest. We will never know exactly how many people were killed because they wanted to continue to live their lives according to

V. The Forgotten Knowledge of the four Elements

their 'heretical' or 'pagan' beliefs. The truth is that many died and those who survived had to pass on their understandings in secret. An oral tradition needs continuity and a degree of social stability in order to thrive. If key teachers are suddenly lost before they have a chance to pass on their wisdom, they would have each taken some of their understandings to the grave and their spiritual lineage would have begun its process of fragmentation.

Even though the persecution lasted for several centuries, some information was successfully encrypted and a surprising amount has survived. The knowledge that we have inherited has been encoded, hidden or disguised, giving rise to our cultural treasury of myth, legend and fairy tale. Some aspects of the original teachings became rather jumbled and other fragments were lost but we have continued to be fascinated by the various symbols, metaphors and allusions that have been handed down in the myths and tales of the past. This suggests that the original archetypal powers that lie behind the various stories continue to live in spite of their message being disguised. Even though some distortions have crept in over time, we continue to intuitively feel the underlying truth and its relevance to our lives today.

VI. Chrétien's Story of Perceval and the Holy Grail

AT FIRST SIGHT, THE VARIOUS STORIES THAT MAKE UP the Grail tradition can seem rather confusing due to the number of threads that make up this complex tapestry of reality and myth. I suspect that this is partly because the original, oral tradition was added to, or overlaid by, the events of Christ's story of Underworld Initiation (the Crucifixion) as well as the fact that the written legacy dates from a time when, due to persecution, a significant degree of coding and encryption was already necessary.

The authors such as Chrétien de Troyes and Wolfram von Eschenberg, writing in the 12th century, were clearly trying to weave a Christian overlay through what is essentially a pre-Christian tradition, presumably, in part, to make the links between the two systems. I find that it helps to bear in mind that these poets were writing for their times and in ways which would have made sense to the people of their culture. I also feel that they were indirectly making comments about the social issues of the day as well as trying to transmit their spiritual understandings.

VI. Chrétien's Story of Perceval and the Holy Grail

The earlier, Celtic stories that relate to the Grail tradition, such as 'The Mabinogion' and the poems of Taliesin, have a very different flavour to them because they reflect the pre-Christian and very early Celtic-Christian tradition. In these tales, the motifs of the older tradition are much more obvious when the basic pattern of the symbolism is understood.

In his book, *Healing the Wounded King*, John Matthews tells us that the earliest text that deals explicitly with the quest for the Holy Grail was written around 1220, by Chrétien de Troyes. This account was in the form of a long poem and it was titled, *Perceval, or the Story of the Grail*. This was Chrétien's last work and it is assumed that he died before he could complete it. In the event, several other authors added to it and over the next 200 years or so, various other versions also appeared. Although many aspects of the central story stayed more or less the same, the later additions and variations have certainly added to the confusion of details that we are left with today.

I am going to concentrate on Chrétien's version of the Grail story because it was the original and he was the first to use the term 'Holy Grail'. Even so, there are a few later 'embellishments' which I feel are worth mentioning because their symbolic comments seem to be just as important today as they must have been nearly 800 years ago. I am particularly referring to the link between Joseph of Arimathea and the Grail legend.

One of the later additions to Chrétien's poem tells us that the bleeding spear or lance that appears during the

VI. Chrétien's Story of Perceval and the Holy Grail

procession of mysterious objects that Perceval sees in the house of the Fisher King, is none other than the one which was used by the centurion, Longinus, to pierce the side of Christ when He was on the cross. Also, the Grail is described as being the cup that Christ used at the Last Supper. In some stories this cup was used later by Joseph of Arimathea to collect the blood of Christ which flowed from the wound made by the spear when He was taken down from the cross and placed in the tomb. The legend is that Joseph brought this sacred cup or chalice with him when he left the Holy Land and travelled to Glastonbury in England, a number of years after the Crucifixion.

We may never know if Joseph's journey was a historical reality so his arrival will probably remain in the realm of myth, but there is still the symbolic message. It does seem very likely that the first Christian church was established in Britain in Glastonbury. Later, the abbey became one of the largest and most important centres of the Christian faith in Britain before it was destroyed by King Henry VIII during the Dissolution of the Monasteries. Somehow, with the abbey reduced to ruins, Glastonbury has kept its reputation as a centre of spiritual pilgrimage and people of many faiths come from all over the world to enjoy its particular sense of palpable mystery.

At first sight, Chrétien's story of Perceval and the Grail appears quite complicated and almost confusing. There are a lot of seemingly inconsequential events that don't immediately make much sense and it is easy to

VI. Chrétien's Story of Perceval and the Holy Grail

dismiss some of the details as nonsense. When I came to look at it, I was already familiar with the symbolic themes of the Underworld Initiation through working with the stories of Isis and Inanna but I had to also delve deeply into the Celtic tradition of Cerridwen and Taliesin before I could decipher some of Chrétien's highly coded symbolism.

In the end, I found the weaving of symbolism and metaphor in Perceval's story absolutely fascinating and very clever. I feel certain that Chrétien was writing to preserve the legacy of the Black Madonna in an extremely uncertain political climate when the leaders of the Christian Church were starting to become very threatened by the ancient wisdom of the 'old religion'.

The very real threat of persecution made Chrétien extremely inventive. He could not use too many symbols that were obvious links with the Underworld tradition because that would have made his message far too blatant. Instead he managed to find a way of including some very clever twists in his story as well as using plays on words and meanings which appear at first to be inconsequential but are actually highly significant. I suspect that this is why he was the first to use the term 'Holy Grail', a delightful touch of poetic licence that manages to allude to both the Celtic and the Christian traditions at the same time without completely giving the game away. The fact that these two tantalising words have managed to intrigue the imagination of thousands of people for over 800 years bears testament to his deep understanding of the

VI. Chrétien's Story of Perceval and the Holy Grail

human psyche and his consummate skill as a writer.

We first meet Perceval when he is a young man. He has grown up in relative isolation with his widowed mother, in their home, deep in the heart of the Waste Forest. At this point in the story, Perceval is not even aware of his true name. He had two older brothers, but, together with his father, they have already died as knights in battle and his mother protects Perceval from this knowledge. She is afraid that Perceval will want to become a knight and be killed as well so she keeps him in ignorance of the King's court and knight's world of battle and chivalry. This means that Perceval has to teach himself how to hunt wild animals for food but, we are told, as he grows up, he becomes highly skilled, especially with the javelin or spear.

One day, in the woods, Perceval suddenly meets some knights who are out hunting. He is overawed by them. He does not know whether they are demons or angels because, in his simple life in the forest, he has never seen anyone dressed in glittering armour and riding such magnificent horses. He falls to his knees and begs them to tell him where they are from. The knights explain that they come from King Arthur's court and then they go on their way.

Perceval goes home to his mother but he is filled with the desire to leave the forest and find his way to King Arthur's court. He cannot forget the powerful knights in their shining armour and he wants to become one of them. His mother is dismayed and tries to put him off, but, in the end, she relents and accepts

VI. Chrétien's Story of Perceval and the Holy Grail

that he must leave home to find his fortune. She knows that he is still completely ignorant about women, that he knows nothing of the knights' codes of conduct and the ways of the world, so she offers him some advice. Although he hears her, he is much too excited to fully listen.

Perceval's mother tells him that he should offer to help if he ever meets a woman in distress and that if such a woman offers him a kiss in return, then he should accept it. She also tells him that a woman's favours should never be taken by force and that if he is ever offered a ring, then it should be accepted because it was usually a sign of friendship, trust or good faith.

As Perceval leaves his mother, he looks back to see her fainting by the doorway of her house but he is keen to get on with his journey so he carries on. After riding for a while, he comes to a fine pavilion at the side of the road. Going inside, he finds a beautiful girl and a table laid out with wine and food. He only half remembers his mother's advice about what to do if he meets a woman, so, in his confusion, he gets everything wrong and behaves very badly. Without asking, he steals a kiss from the girl. He then increases her distress by demanding the ring that she is wearing on her finger. Before he leaves, he helps himself to the wine and food that is spread out on the table.

Perceval resumes his journey and soon arrives at the King's palace. As he enters the gates, he meets a knight dressed in red armour. As the knight rushes past him, Perceval notices that he is carrying a golden cup. When

VI. Chrétien's Story of Perceval and the Holy Grail

Perceval goes into the court he finds out that the Red Knight has stolen the golden cup after insulting King Arthur and spilling wine over the Queen.

Perceval announces to the court that he is prepared to go after the Red Knight and avenge this outrage but straight away his offer is mocked and ridiculed by Sir Kay, King Arthur's chief steward. One of the maidens in the court, a quiet and serious girl who has not laughed for a long time, surprises everyone by suddenly announcing a prophesy that this unknown youth would one day be famous. Sir Kay hits the girl for what he regards as insolent behaviour.

Perceval leaves the court and goes after the Red Knight. After fighting with him, the Red Knight is killed and Perceval can therefore claim the dead man's armour, together with his weapons and his war horse. So, after putting on his newly acquired armour and getting onto the defeated knight's horse, Perceval continues with his journey and later arrives at another castle. This castle is owned by an older knight named Gorneman. Gorneman is so impressed with Perceval's story of defeating the Red Knight that he offers to teach Perceval the skills of war, chivalry and knighthood. Perceval is a good pupil and he is quick to learn, so, in due course, Gorneman makes him a knight.

It is not long before Perceval becomes restless again, being eager to continue with his adventures. Before he leaves the castle, Gorneman offers him some further advice, this being to help those in need, to learn not to talk too much and to refrain from asking too many

VI. Chrétien's Story of Perceval and the Holy Grail

questions because people might think that he is foolish or mad. Thanking him, Perceval goes on his way.

After a while, Perceval comes to a town with a castle. He finds out that the lands are owned by a beautiful maiden called Blanchfleur but she and her people are being besieged by the knight, Engygeron, who is determined to force Blanchfleur into marrying him. Blanchfleur's lands have been laid to waste and the whole town is ruined. Perceval is determined to help and with his new skills as a knight, he quickly defeats Engygeron. Blanchfleur is released from persecution and her lands are restored to her.

When Perceval meets Blanchfleur they immediately fall in love with each other but as Perceval opens his heart to love, he is reminded of his mother and he realises that he has been gone from home for a long time. He remembers that the last time that he saw his mother she was fainting at the doorway of her house. He realises that he must go home and make sure that his mother is all right and tell her all about his adventures. Blanchfleur does not want to lose him but she knows that she cannot stop him leaving. Perceval wastes no time and soon sets off to return to his home in the forest.

He quickly loses his way in the thick woodland and when he comes to a deep, fiercely flowing stretch of river, he becomes frightened because he can't see a way of crossing it. Seeing a man fishing calmly from a small boat in the centre of the river, Perceval calls out, asking for a way to cross. The man calls back saying that there

VI. Chrétien's Story of Perceval and the Holy Grail

is nowhere nearby where Perceval can ford the river but he is welcome to stay overnight at the fisherman's house instead.

Perceval follows the fisherman's instructions. He follows the bank of the river upstream, gradually climbing to find a cleft in the rocks at the rugged summit of a hill, just as described by the fisherman. As Perceval looks down into the valley below, he sees the tower of a beautiful manor house, half hidden by the surrounding trees. When he reaches the manor, he goes inside where he is welcomed by the servants. He is shown into a large hall where he finds an elderly man, the lord of the household, sitting upright in a large bed. The old lord invites Perceval to come and sit near to him so that they can talk. After a while, a young man comes into the hall carrying a special, jewelled sword. The old lord declares that the sword is destined to belong to Perceval as he fastens it onto his guest.

The two men carry on talking. A bit later, another youth comes in, carrying a white lance. Perceval watches in astonishment as a drop of blood starts to emerge from the tip of the lance before running down the shaft. He wants to ask why this is happening but he says nothing because he remembers Gorneman's advice about not asking too many questions in case he looks stupid.

Two more young men then come into the hall, each one carrying a golden candelabrum bearing ten candles. They are followed by a girl carrying a large silver serving dish. Finally, another girl comes in. She is

VI. Chrétien's Story of Perceval and the Holy Grail

carrying a magnificent golden Grail covered in the most wonderful jewels. A dazzling light shines from the Grail, so bright that it makes the candles seem quite dim. All these treasures are carried past Perceval, but he is still reluctant to ask about their meaning so he says nothing. He resolves that he will ask a servant about them in the morning.

After dining, the old lord is carried to his bedchamber and Perceval sleeps on the bed that is in the middle of the great hall. In the morning, he awakes to find that the whole manor house is deserted – the lord and all his servants have disappeared. He does find his clothes and armour laid out ready for him and his horse waiting outside, but no one answers his calls so he cannot ask about the mysterious objects that he saw the previous night. Deeply perplexed, Perceval leaves but he is not sure of where to go next. He follows some fresh tracks in the hope that they might be those of the lord and his servants.

The tracks lead to a maiden who is crying at the side of the pathway. The body of her dead lover is next to her at the edge of the track. Distracted by the sudden appearance of Perceval, the maiden asks him where he has come from. When he explains about the manor house nearby where he stayed the night, the maiden tells Perceval that the old lord of the castle is the wounded Fisher King. After being injured in the thigh in a battle, the Fisher King can no longer ride. The maiden explains that the injury is severe and very incapacitating and the Fisher King has spent many

VI. Chrétien's Story of Perceval and the Holy Grail

years suffering because of it. She seems to know all about the manor house and she wants to know if Perceval was shown the spear and the other miraculous objects and whether he asked what they were for. Perceval says that he did see them but he has to admit that he had failed to ask any questions about them.

This answer makes the maiden angry with Perceval and she tells him that he has been stupid for not asking about the meaning of the Grail, the bleeding lance and the other objects. She explains that if he had only asked about these mysteries, then the Fisher King would have been healed of his terrible wound, that he could have then returned to his former position as the King and that his people would no longer have to live in a wasteland.

The maiden goes on to tell Perceval that she knows who he really is. She tells him his name and then she informs him that she is his cousin and that she used to live with him and his mother when he was a young baby. She also says that his mother had died of sorrow when he left her behind because she had thought that he would die on his journey.

Perceval is greatly distressed with shame and grief when he receives all of this information. He offers to redeem himself by finding the knight who has killed the maiden's lover. In reply, the maiden warns him to be careful because the sword that he was given by the Fisher King is liable to break when he is in most need of it, but Perceval is still keen to redress the balance and he sets off to find the offending knight at once.

VI. Chrétien's Story of Perceval and the Holy Grail

He soon meets a woman on the pathway. She is dressed in a ruined dress and she is riding an old and exhausted horse. Perceval realises that this is the girl who he first met years before when he had just set out on his journey. This woman was the girl that he had found in the pavilion, the one who he had robbed of her ring and clumsily kissed. He talks to her and she tells him that her lover has been punishing her ever since that day when Perceval had forced himself onto her because her lover was very jealous. Her punishment is to ride in front of her lover in rags and on a worn out horse.

At this point, the woman's lover, the Jealous Knight, actually arrives on the scene. Perceval realises that the Jealous Knight is also the one who has killed the lover of the maiden, his cousin. Perceval challenges the Jealous Knight to a duel. Perceval quickly wins the fight even though his beautiful sword gets broken in the process. Perceval makes the Jealous Knight promise to return to the court where King Arthur can make a judgement that will redress the suffering of the punishment that he has been giving to his lover for years.

The Jealous Knight keeps his promise and goes to King Arthur's court to receive punishment. This is how King Arthur comes to hear of Perceval's exploits. The King is impressed and he sets out with a company of knights to find the gallant Perceval.

Perceval knows nothing of this because he has continued on his way through the forest. Suddenly he

VI. Chrétien's Story of Perceval and the Holy Grail

sees a wild goose being attacked by a hawk. The blood of the goose falls on the snow-covered ground and the contrast of the red blood on the white snow shocks Perceval into the memory of Blanchfleur's beautiful face with its pale skin and rosy cheeks. He becomes so completely lost in this memory that he doesn't realise what is happening around him when King Arthur's knights find him.

Sir Kay is in the group of knights and, recognising the younger knight, Sir Kay rides up to speak with Perceval. Perceval, however, is still completely entranced by the sight of red blood on the white snow. When Sir Kay approaches him, Perceval unconsciously lashes out, knocking the other man from his horse with his blow. Sir Kay breaks his arm as he falls from his horse. Eventually Perceval frees himself from the spell of his memory of Blanchfleur and he is able to greet King Arthur and ride triumphantly back with him to the court.

This time of celebration does not last for very long. At court the next day, a hideous old woman arrives on a mule. She is the most ugly creature that anyone has ever seen. She has wild, black hair that hangs in snake-like tresses, tiny black eyes like a rat and a small nose like a cat. Her teeth are yellow, she has a beard like a goat, her body is twisted and her legs are deformed. In spite of this, the hideous old woman rides boldly into the centre of the court and she greets everyone except Perceval.

Perceval does not get a greeting from the loathly hag. Instead, she turns on him, cursing and berating

VI. Chrétien's Story of Perceval and the Holy Grail

him. She is furious because he has been stupid for not asking about the bleeding lance and the Grail when he was given the opportunity. Again he is reminded that if he had only had the wit to ask about the wounded Fisher King and the meaning of the service of the Grail, then a great healing would have happened and the King would have been restored to health along with the fertility of his lands and his people. The loathly hag tells Perceval that now, because he dared not ask the vital question, there will be more distress, that the Fisher King's kingdom will be further laid to waste and many of his people will now die or be killed.

The loathly hag then begins to announce a whole series of challenges and adventures for the other knights to attempt. Perceval, meanwhile, is mortified by her angry words and the fact that he could have done something to help the wounded Fisher King. Perceval swears that he will not rest until he has found out about the meaning of the mysterious objects and the service of the Grail. Immediately, Perceval leaves the court. He goes back into the forest to search for the house of the Fisher King.

At this point, Chrétien's story becomes a bit vague about what happens to Perceval. We are told that he spends the next five years wandering in the wilderness of the forest, intent on keeping to his oath of not resting until he has found the house of the Fisher King and the meaning of the lance and the Grail. From time to time he comes across errant knights and sends them back to King Arthur's court, but he never finds the manor

VI. Chrétien's Story of Perceval and the Holy Grail

house and, in time, his wandering becomes aimless because he has forgotten what he was looking for.

His story resumes when we are told that it is Good Friday. Perceval comes across a procession of knights and ladies in the forest. They are all hooded, barefoot, and without their armour because they are walking in pilgrimage and mourning for the sacrifice of the Crucifixion of the Lord Christ. Perceval has been wandering in the Waste Forest on his own for so long that he has no idea what time of the year it is and he is wearing his weapons and armour in the usual way. The knights are surprised to see another knight bearing arms during a religious festival and they remind Perceval that it is coming up to the mysteries of the festival of Easter and that a knight should lay down his weapons and take off his armour at this special time.

Perceval asks the people where they have come from and they say that they have been visiting a holy hermit who lives in a chapel close by. Perceval is shocked as he realises that he has completely lost his way and that he has even forgotten the purpose of his quest. He decides, therefore, to visit the hermit so that he can ask for his blessings and forgiveness.

When he reaches the hermit's chapel, Perceval falls on his knees and weeps for a long time. He confesses the whole of his long, sad story as the hermit listens carefully. The hermit then tells Perceval that they are relatives and that he is actually Perceval's uncle, his mother's brother. He also explains that even though the Fisher King was also another of Perceval's uncles, Perceval was not ready

VI. Chrétien's Story of Perceval and the Holy Grail

to ask about the meaning of the Grail because, at that time, he was prevented from knowing because of his unacknowledged grief about the death of his mother.

Perceval weeps some more as he begins to understand the full truth of his situation. The hermit forgives him and suggests that he can now participate in the Mass of Good Friday and receive the Holy Sacraments. After this, he will be able to rest.

This seems to be the end of Chrétien's story of Perceval though there are some additions and other versions that were written by later writers. It could be argued that because the story is incomplete, Perceval must have failed in the last part of his Underworld Initiation because it seems as though he never found the house of the Fisher King and the meaning of the Grail, but I would like to suggest another possibility.

The Grail, as a symbol of the recognition and conscious reconnection with the soul, the inner aspect of spiritual consciousness, is a highly subjective experience. It is a private change or shift in awareness that is not necessarily recognised on the 'outside' except, perhaps, by another successful initiate. In his story, Chrétien makes a very clear link between the timing of the mysteries of the transformation and rebirth of the Crucifixion and Resurrection of Christ at Easter, with Perceval's process of grieving and redemption as he confesses his story and then hears the truth of his life journey from the hermit.

The events of the Crucifixion of Christ, as they are described in the Bible, are a classic portrayal of the final

VI. Chrétien's Story of Perceval and the Holy Grail

processes of the Underworld Initiation leading up to the 'rebirth', or transformation of consciousness that happens after three days of lying inert in the tomb. When Perceval surrenders, repents and sacrifices his sins, he receives forgiveness for the omissions of his ignorance. He would then have gone into the chapel to receive the Holy Sacraments, this being the outward enactment of the inner transformation in consciousness which is at the heart of the mystery of the inner spiritual processes of forgiveness, reconnection and redemption. We are told that this all happened on Good Friday so there would have been three days of 'rest' before Perceval's 'rebirth' on Easter Sunday. I would like to think that Chrétien wanted us to know that Perceval *did* receive the teachings of the service of the Grail as he rested in the sanctuary of the hermit's tiny chapel even though he never had the chance to say a word about it!

VII. The Message of the Grail

LIKE ALL ENDURING MYTHS, THERE ARE MANY LAYERS OF symbolism encoded within Chrétien's story of Perceval's search for the Grail. The characters and events represent the various stages of Perceval's spiritual growth as they are reflected back to him through his interactions with others. Other incidents and descriptions do not make sense unless it is assumed that Chrétien was also commenting on another, more collective, spiritual issue, as this weaves through the intricate fabric of his story.

Chrétien's tale is a kind of early form of literary novel. He manages to describe his hero's inner challenges and spiritual experiences within the context of the social climate of his day whilst also commenting on the religious and political malaise which had started to affect both the individual and the collective consciousness of his time. He must have understood the human condition very well because he underlines the truth that many of the thoughts and beliefs of an individual are influenced or forged from the social paradigm of their particular time and place until a point in spiritual awareness is reached where it is possible to see through this overlay and become free of the negative repercussions of its influence.

VII. The Message of the Grail

Chrétien was not content with just pointing out the political issues that were developing in his culture; he wanted to go further and offer solutions. With this in mind, he makes his observations and then subtly encodes the ancient wisdom that will correct the problem. He had to do this cleverly and carefully. Pointing out that those in positions of authority are starting to misuse their power and then also revealing how they are getting away with it, usually runs the risk of some kind of censure.

Chrétien had to disguise what he was saying without compromising his message and he does this very skilfully. By the end of his story, he has presented the misuse of power that was evolving within the emerging hierarchy of the Christian Church with its energetic cause as well as the personal and collective repercussions. He then presents the spiritual solution in a way that still has the power to speak to the intuitive psyche over 800 years later.

It is likely that Chrétien was an initiate of the Underworld mysteries of the Goddess, the ancient wisdom of the Celtic people which became the secrets of the Black Madonna. This was the prevailing spiritual belief system that existed in most of Europe before a frightened and power-hungry Church hierarchy labelled it heretic or the work of the devil and relentlessly persecuted its ancient legacy. The full name of Chrétien's hero is Perceval le Gallois, the name Gallois being variously translated as 'Welsh' or 'Gaul'. The word Gaul comes from the Roman name for the Celtic

VII. The Message of the Grail

people who lived in the area of Europe that later became part of France and there were strong ancestral connections between the people living Wales, the South-west of England and the southern areas of France.

The Underworld teachings include the understanding that we all have an immortal soul which reincarnates a number of times in the process of learning how to lovingly use the powers of the four Elements, these being the energetic qualities of pre-matter, the essential keys to the mastery of the laws of creativity as they manifest themselves on the physical levels of existence. This knowledge includes a deep understanding of the moral dilemmas of the psyche as it gradually develops and grows towards an enlightened comprehension of the true nature of the human condition.

Chrétien obviously had these understandings. He must have realised that growing persecution might lead to a loss of this ancient knowledge so he cleverly encoded the teachings of the Black Goddess and the Underworld Initiation into the apparent innocence of his tale. His intuition proved to be right. We now know that this wisdom came very close to vanishing but Chrétien and others like him had left enough clues and it is possible to reassemble a jigsaw puzzle when you know what you are looking for in the design.

The answer that is embodied in Chrétien's icon of the Holy Grail is not a cure-all or panacea. Its message has to be embraced by the individual first before the gestalt of a culture can reach critical mass and make a

VII. The Message of the Grail

lasting change in the collective psyche. The past will always be repeated if the individual continues to subconsciously mimic those who have already usurped the sovereignty of moral conscience, the personal integrity of spiritual authority, by any act of force or deviousness. All enforced, authoritarian dogma is an abuse of the Elemental powers of air and fire so the individual has to make a personal commitment to quest for the truth by consciously changing their own negative patterns of misuse of these powers when they are discovered in the personal psyche.

After 800 years, the icon of the Grail continues to fascinate because it is a potent symbol of the loving guidance of the wisdom of the hidden soul, the solution to healing the spiritual wounding that we all need to address at some level. The sword of truth must be taken up first to bring clarity to the dilemma but insight on its own is not enough. Genuine transformation can only happen when the creative powers of the feminine Elements are returned to a psyche that has evolved a destructive and over-masculine mix, something which the mediaeval alchemists were trying to explain. As the qualities of earth and water are retrieved and reaffirmed, their healing balm brings balance to their masculine counterparts so that the child of a new personal and collective way of being can be born. This was the knowledge that came close to being lost but the Black Madonnas remain to stir our sleeping memories.

VII. The Message of the Grail

1. An Open Mind

The story begins with Perceval as boy or youth. He has grown up in relative isolation in the Waste Forest with only his mother to advise and teach him so he is clearly made out to be an archetypal innocent, the naive 'fool' who still has an open mind at the beginning of his spiritual life's journey. Perceval's knowledge of the ways of the world is limited to what his mother has told him and what he has managed to work out for himself. Later on in the story, it becomes obvious that his innocence proves to be both a blessing and a curse but we can also understand that our hero is resourceful with a practical intelligence because we are told that he has already taught himself the skills necessary to hunt.

I find it fascinating that Chrétien actually calls the forest itself the 'Waste Forest'. This obviously ties in with the mysterious Fisher King, the mysterious Lord of the Wasteland who we meet later on in the story. A bit of background to this fascinating nugget of information supports the sense of there being many layers of symbol and metaphor that the story 'innocently' carries.

In the pre-Christian, Celtic and Druid traditions of Europe, one of the important Goddess figures was the Dark Mother. She had many aspects and associations, being best known, perhaps, as Cerridwen, the Crone Mother of the Underworld. Cerridwen guarded a huge cauldron, thought to be one of the early symbols that relate to the mysterious Grail. This magical cauldron

VII. The Message of the Grail

offered many gifts, including those of transformation, rebirth and regeneration. It was also a symbol of the other, more primeval powers of Mother Earth, having the ability to withhold the fertility of the land, something which, in time, would lead to the land and all its people, plants, animals and birds, becoming barren, and hence a wasteland. So, by calling the wood that Perceval grows up in, the Waste Forest, Chrétien is able to allude to the whole of the ancient, pre-Christian tradition of the feminine mysteries of the Goddess in just two words. As the story progresses, the ancient wisdom of the Dark Goddess weaves in and out of the story as its relevance to Perceval's quest is gradually revealed.

Chrétien also tells us that Perceval's mother is widowed and that she is bringing her son up on her own. Again this detail might seem inconsequential. It is a common enough situation and it probably happened as much in the 12th century as it does today but there is another allusion hinted in the carefree line, the 'son of the widow'. This goes back to – guess who? – Isis herself! In the Egyptian tradition much is made of the fact that Isis has to bring up her son, Horus, on her own after her husband, Osiris, is cruelly dismembered by his evil brother Seth. Later, these simple words became a sort of coded catchphrase which the Knights Templar used to signify the esoteric information that they had rediscovered in the Middle East when they were out and about on their Crusades.

Perceval's father and brothers were knights but they

VII. The Message of the Grail

are all dead, killed in battle. In this time period, the status of knighthood would have been a highly honourable social achievement, an aspiration for every young man. A knight would have needed to have a wide range of skills and abilities including financial resources or a benefactor, physical strength and prowess, as well as a knowledge of social etiquette and the moral manners and behavioural codes of the King's court.

In this time period, each knight would have taken oaths that were a part of the code of chivalry, an agreed system of 'fair play' in a time when much of Europe was practically lawless, ruled by brute force rather than a legal system based on a sense of justice coming from the law of the land. Unfortunately, becoming a knight was also a way of getting killed and Perceval's mother doesn't want to lose her remaining son to the cut of lance or the blow of a sword's blade, even though this might be sustained in fair combat. She therefore unwittingly adds to Perceval's state of ignorance by resolving to keep him innocent of who he is in terms of his inheritance, background and ancestry.

Perceval's spiritual destiny, however, demands that he leave home and learn more about life so that he can fully develop all of his talents. In the process, he will find out who he really is. So, before his mother's protective boundaries can become too limiting, fate steps in to give him a glimpse of other potentials.

Perceval meets some knights while he is out hunting in the forest. In his ignorance, he does not know who or

VII. The Message of the Grail

what they are but when he finds out, the image of their embodied power fires up his imagination, his longing and his ambition. Perceval suddenly realises that he has other possibilities and he is determined that he shall go to the King's court with the aim of becoming a knight himself. He has glimpsed the understanding that there is something more to life than catching rabbits and although he has no idea what this is, nothing is going to stop him from finding out.

Like most people, Perceval has embarked on his life journey from a state of innocence. He has no real idea of what he is doing and how he is going to do it. As he is leaving his mother, she offers him some advice so he will know how to behave with other people. Her words are obviously very specific to their time period and while the details may sound quite amusing to us today, there are some important messages encoded in the way that they are given nonetheless.

The trouble is that Perceval is so excited about his coming adventure that he can't listen properly to his mother and because he doesn't have a context in which he can understand what she is saying, a bit later on, he gets it all wrong. This leads to some important repercussions that he has to deal with later when his past catches up with him towards the end of the story. Nothing much has changed here then: when did any teenager think that it was worth listening to their mother!

His mother's advice is specific to Perceval's future dealings with women. Throughout the story, there is a

VII. The Message of the Grail

layer of encoded information that relates to the four Elements as their powers weave in and out of the various situations that happen to Perceval as he is tested through the events of his journey. One of the key understandings relates to the way that these Elemental qualities pair up together as masculine and feminine polarities, earth and water being the feminine powers while fire and air represent their masculine counterparts. This means that the threads that run through the tale that reference Perceval's interactions and relationships with the various male and female characters are actually a crucial part of the story because they reveal his evolving mastery of the Elemental powers of manifestation and spiritual growth.

While we can learn much about life from developing our own natural abilities, a vital part of everyone's learning experience comes from the ordinary day-to-day interactions that occur with the other people around us. We are often naturally attracted to those who have either a greater skill, more life experience or another kind of innate talent that we don't yet possess. This means that we may want to form relationships with other people who can act as role models for us so that we can learn more about their particular abilities.

These kinds of essential learning experiences do not always come in the form of a conventional teacher—pupil relationship. We learn a massive amount of lessons about the powers of the four Elements through the natural exchanges of energies that are a part of the ordinary dynamics that happen in all our romantic

VII. The Message of the Grail

relationships. We are attracted to a mate for biological reasons of course, but even this interaction will offer us teachings about the nature of our 'opposite' Elemental polarity, just through the process of interacting with our beloved.

Here, at the beginning of the story, Perceval hasn't got a clue about the importance of needing to learn how to relate in a balanced, sharing, giving and receiving kind of way to his opposite polarity, that is, a woman. His mother therefore tries to help him by explaining some basic understandings. Her instructions are probably based on the codes of chivalry of the time, which is why they sound rather old-fashioned in the context of the social mores of today but, as I understand it, they are trying to communicate a fundamental attitude of honour and respect towards the feminine Elemental virtues, something which is becoming sadly lacking in many relationships today.

It seems as though Perceval just can't understand what his mother is saying or that he is not able to really listen. When he actually leaves her behind, he appears to be completely wrapped up in himself and his ambitions for the future, a common enough failing in the young! When he sees his mother fall down, he does not even consider going back to see what has happened to her. Perceval's mother is the first personification of the feminine Elemental energies that he encounters but, apparently, at this point in the story, he seems to have absolutely no idea about the need to relate to the feminine polarity at all.

VII. The Message of the Grail

We find out later on in the story that Perceval did love his mother and that he really cared a lot for her, but by this time it is too late to express it because she is dead. In a sense, this one simple incident encapsulates one of the key issues of the whole story – the capacity of the energy polarity of the masculine Elements to cut out, deny or consciously suppress any kind of appreciation of the equal function and value of its 'opposite', the powers of the feminine principle.

I suspect that many modern women continue to secretly long for a knight in shining armour, even though, in the days of female emancipation, this is seen as being extremely politically incorrect or unacceptable. I also suspect that there is an archetypal truth to this closet fantasy because the vision of such a knight symbolically represents the balanced expression of the male Elemental qualities, a strong man who is also sensitive and has a genuine respect and honour for the positive qualities of the archetypal feminine, the 'flower', that is still hidden in the heart of every woman, in spite of Women's Lib.

When Perceval sets out to find his way to King Arthur's court, he is setting off on his life quest of becoming fully spiritually conscious of who he really is. We later find out that he doesn't actually know his name at this early stage in his journey and this is another indication of the deeper message behind the story. Perceval literally does not know who he is. In a sense, this fact is also part of his saving grace because in his innocent, nameless, 'fatherless' state, he still has enough openness of mind and heart to allow him the freedom to keep searching for the truth of the purpose of his life until he finds it.

In our modern culture, we have forgotten that every name has a magical or spiritual meaning and that this meaning, in itself, has power. In many tribal societies, knowing your spiritual name and claiming its power is an important part of owning the karmic purpose of the current lifetime as well as the truth of who you are on the soul level of being. The name 'Perceval' has a number of related forms such as 'Parsifal', 'Peredur' and 'Perlesvaus' and the root of these names has several possible meanings. The various forms of his name are thought to translate as 'pierce the valley', 'pierce the veil' or 'self-made' respectively.[9]

Although he does not realise it, from now on, every event in the course of Perceval's quest will be either a part of his process of acquiring a greater command or skill of an Elemental power or a test of his current level of proficiency. Under the guise of the encounters with the various other people along his journey, he will face many of the ways that the various Elemental qualities can be used; so, sequentially, he faces the tests and challenges of learning about these different powers in both their positive/creative aspects, as well as their negative/destructive aspects.

When he realises, in retrospect, that he has used a power negatively, with misuse or denial of its real

---

[9] www.baby-names.adoption.com.

VII. The Message of the Grail

value or function, Perceval has to make amends so that he can demonstrate, through a direct action, that he knows what to do to redress the imbalance and not repeat the same mistake or 'sin', again.

2. The Challenges and Tests of the Four Elemental Empowerments

Perceval's first test comes almost immediately. Having just left his mother behind, Perceval is soon challenged again in terms of relating to his opposite, inner feminine function. When he finds the girl in the pavilion, he can't remember his mother's advice properly so he rashly jumps in, gets it all wrong and ends up, in today's terms, abusing the girl. At this point, Perceval has no understanding of how to give and receive energies on any kind of equal basis. He demonstrates this in taking the girl's honour when he 'steals' a kiss, taking her ring by force and by helping himself to her wine and food. Chrétien embodies the whole issue of the individual and collective attitude towards the feminine Elemental powers with this rather comic but highly symbolic medley of exploitation, misuse and abuse.

This event comes back to haunt Perceval later when he meets the girl again, but this time he is able to make amends and actively redress the imbalance. This act of retribution comes towards the end of the story as an indication of just how much Perceval has learnt in the course of his journey.

Perceval's next test relates to the masculine side of

VII. The Message of the Grail

his personality. When he reaches King Arthur's castle, he encounters the Red Knight who is leaving with a golden cup. Perceval enters the court and learns that the Red Knight has just insulted the King and Queen as well as stealing the cup. He is quick to see how he can avenge these insults and also further his ambitions at the same time. He goes after the Red Knight, challenges him to a duel and kills him. In this way, Perceval acquires a warhorse, a set of weapons and a suit of armour, all symbols of masculine Elemental empowerments.

The errant Red Knight can be seen as a personification of the negative qualities of the masculine powers, particularly the fire Element. The fire Element is the principle of action and initiative but, unchecked, it can be impulsive, selfish and completely inconsiderate of others. Seeing something it wants, negative fire can act like the complete egomaniac who thoughtlessly plunders and raids without any concern for the outcome of its actions. In this mode, there is no consideration about the feelings (water) or resources (earth) of others. This incident hints at another issue that Chrétien weaves through his story: the importance of becoming aware of how the Elemental powers are being used, in particular – the fire Element.

The powers of the other three Elements can also be used in negative ways, of course, but Chrétien's penetrating insight is that it is the fire Element that has the ability to be the most destructive and hurtful when its energies are used negatively. This makes sense when it

VII. The Message of the Grail

is understood that fire represents the power to take an initiative or creative action. One of the misuses or abuses of this power includes the ability to actively prevent another person from taking an initiative action.

We can think (air) about killing ourselves or others but the results of executing this action (fire), can be, quite literally, deadly. The other important quality of the fire Element includes the function of increasing spiritual perception as it relates to judging the moral consequences or results of an action. We learn or increase our consciousness by making judgements or evaluations of the results of our creative actions and this has the effect of gradually increasing our spiritual consciousness as a unique human being.

This means that if someone manages to stop another individual from taking a creative initiative, they are, in effect, sabotaging the spiritual growth of the other person. The 'sabotaged' person will intuitively recognise this because they will feel anger towards the bully, anger being the feeling of the frustrated or negative 'spin' of the energy of creativity. Another way that one person can inflict negative fire energy onto another is to try and 'shame or blame' them because this is a judgement taken on behalf of another person, shame being the feeling of having done something that you should not do, an action that is judged to be somehow harmful towards another.

Perceval demonstrates the fact that he understands that the Red Knight's actions towards the King and Queen have been shameful and he is quick to redress

VII. The Message of the Grail

the knight's insulting behaviour when he offers to challenge the knight to a duel. This is a good opportunity for Perceval because it also gives him a chance to prove himself, 'earn his spurs', or test his new masculine powers. When we are told that Perceval kills the Red Knight, we can only assume that in the culture of his times, this behaviour was regarded as a 'fair cop'. There is the hint that Perceval has only just made the grade because Chrétien adds the detail that he has some difficulty getting the armour off the dead knight but that he does manage it in the end. Thus, Perceval claims his new level of masculine empowerment as he puts on the armour, takes up the weapons and mounts the dead knight's warhorse. Fully equipped as a fledgling knight, he is ready to continue his journey.

He soon arrives at another castle, this being owned by the older, more experienced knight called Gorneman de Gorhaut. Perceval has struck lucky. He has met a mature, older man, the father figure that he never had. Gorneman is impressed with Perceval's exploits and he is happy to take the young man under his wing.

Gorneman represents a positive role model for the skills and abilities of the masculine Elemental empowerments. In some versions of the story, we find out that Gorneman is Blanchfleur's uncle. He is not critical (negative air) or too competitive (negative fire) with the younger man and he does not try to belittle his achievements (negative fire and air). Instead, Gorneman plays the role of the generous benefactor, (positive fire) as he communicates his knowledge, his

VII. The Message of the Grail

expertise and his information (positive air). Gorneman demonstrates these positive expressions of fire and air as he puts himself in the position of teacher and patron and generously passes on all that he knows.

We are told that Perceval is a quick and willing pupil and this implies that it is easy for him to learn about and then embody the other positive qualities of the masculine polarity. When Perceval receives his knighthood from Gorneman, we can understand that he has achieved a considerable skill in the use of the male Elemental powers and that his basic mastery of these qualities is more or less complete. In today's terms, we might say that Perceval's time with Gorneman has 'made a man of him'.

Chrétien makes it clear that Gorneman is the one who makes Perceval a knight. This was a ritual of initiation, a rite of passage that became a symbol of considerable social standing and honour in a time of great unrest and lawlessness. The word 'chivalry' comes from the French word for horse, 'cheval', but there was more to becoming a knight than learning how to ride a warhorse in a full set of armour. In the ritual of becoming a knight, the candidate had to pledge his honour and swear to a set of rules or code of conduct that included the ideals of fair combat and defence of the weak. This set of ideals and moral standards of behaviour became known as the knightly virtues.

I find it interesting that in the early Christian tradition there was the concept of the four cardinal virtues,

VII. The Message of the Grail

usually defined as prudence, temperance, fortitude and justice. 'Cardinal' is still commonly used in reference to the four points of the compass, the four directions, north, south, east and west. A little research into the origin of the word 'cardinal' reveals that it comes from the Latin, '*cardinalis*', meaning 'important, key, chief or essential',[10] and further back, to the Latin, '*cardo*', which means 'hinge' or 'that which something turns on or depends on'. In early English, 'cardinal' had the meaning of 'pivotal' or 'serving as a hinge'.

Putting this all together, a combined meaning of the word 'cardinal' could be expressed as, 'a key or primary principle, which acts as a hinge on which something else pivots or swings' – a surprisingly good definition of the workings of the Elemental powers! Am I going too far in suggesting that the original knightly virtues might have been based on the cardinal virtues? This would mean that in the Middle Ages, a knight would have sworn on oath to uphold the disciplined, positive and creative use of the four Elemental powers in all his dealings with others for the course of the rest of his life.

If so, the correspondences would be:

- north/ air / justice
- south / water / temperance
- east / fire / fortitude
- west / earth / prudence

---

[10] www.answers.com.

VII. The Message of the Grail

When Perceval is ready to leave, Gorneman offers him one last piece of advice. This is another detail in the story that has some important repercussions later on. Gorneman tells Perceval to offer to help those in need but to learn not to talk too much and to not ask too many questions in case other people think that he is either foolish or mad. Perceval takes this advice to heart and it is the main reason why he dares not ask the Fisher King about the meaning of the Grail when he sees it.

Gorneman's advice is an example of a negative or fearful expression of the air Element because it concerns communication and information. I am sure that Gorneman was well meaning so I think that it is meant to represent another of Chrétien's insights into the way negative beliefs, fears and prejudices of a society can be passed down from one generation to another, negatively influencing the mind of the individual and affecting their behaviour in situations where a fearful, socially prescribed behaviour is not useful or appropriate.

Earlier, when Perceval was younger and more innocent, he has no fear about being thought foolish or silly. With the naïve, open charm of youth, he is ready to attempt more or less anything and take on anyone. He challenges the more experienced Red Knight because he just wants to have a go and there is nothing for him to lose in terms of social status or position. Now that he has become a knight, he is a somebody, he has achieved a recognisable level of social proficiency in his culture.

VII. The Message of the Grail

He has also learnt a set of rules and prescribed behaviours that have taken away his spiritual innocence in the process. He will have to pay the price for this later on but, for now, this is the social truth expressed in the events of his archetypal journey. We have to first engage with our culture and learn to play by its rules before we can later develop the inner strength through which we can release ourselves gently from its shackles.

It is now time for Perceval to encounter the 'other', the opposite, 'feminine' half of his psyche in the form of the beautiful maiden, Blanchfleur. Her name means 'White-flower' and she is the embodiment of his inner woman, a previously unconscious aspect of his psyche. This meeting demonstrates that Perceval is now mature enough to fall in love and start to merge with the complementary feminine aspects of his being. This time he passes the test in terms of knowing how to respect, honour and take care of the feminine Elemental powers. He has no reservations when it comes to defending Blanchfleur's honour against the abusive knight who has been holding her and her lands hostage. This kind of war of attrition, incidentally, being another expression of the negative, male, Elemental power trip, the 'if you won't give it to me now then I'll threaten you and take it by force later, if necessary' mode of operating.

Perceval quickly releases Blanchfleur from her state of persecution but he does not stay by her side and live happily ever after in the way of many fairy tales. At first sight, this seems rather odd. He has completely

VII. The Message of the Grail

fallen in love. She, as his 'other half', adores him; she's free to marry and she even has her own property. What more could he want? That Chrétien's story does not stop here suggests that there really is a deeper purpose to his tale.

Perceval's meeting with Blanchfleur is his first fully conscious, loving meeting with the feminine polarity of his psyche. His mother represented his first encounter with these qualities but that was when he was a child and he was too young to understand their importance and value. Again, Chrétien carefully holds his cards to his chest. Although Perceval's relationship with Blanchfleur appears to be brief and apparently inconsequential, it is actually one of the major turning points in the inner workings of Perceval's psyche and hence, his spiritual journey.

In the process of falling in love with our opposite polarity, 'our other half', we are accepting the other person as an embodiment of the Elemental energies that we currently lack or do not yet fully manifest. This offers us the experience of having the other person act these qualities out for us so that we can have the potential of learning, through direct demonstration, just how a particular quality or expertise operates.

This is, of course, an idealised situation, and some of the messiness of most relationships occurs because the partner is not an exact 'fit' in terms of being able or willing to fulfil or supplement the qualities that the other person is lacking. This means that there is the sense of the person failing to deliver in terms of what

VII. The Message of the Grail

we expect from them. Other negative situations can develop if we do not realise that we are meant to support the other person by openly and generously sharing our different skills and abilities. Other imbalances can occur in cases of extreme co-dependency, meaning that one partner becomes so powerless that they cannot function at all without the other person being there.

There are many other negative patterns that can occur in relationships but the key to changing them from negative to positive situations is to regard the whole interaction as an opportunity for learning more about yourself and the various ways that you are using the four Elements. Through a mirroring process, the other person then becomes a teacher as they continually demonstrate or mirror their relative command of these powers by their words and actions.

It does not matter if the other person is a negative teacher in the sense that they are misusing or abusing their Elemental powers, something that the Native American tradition cleverly calls 'the petty tyrant'. With self-compassion, consciousness and courage, it is always possible to learn how to stop giving your power away to a petty tyrant and this means that they will no longer have any power over you. In the process, you learn how you were playing the role of victim and by changing your pattern, there is no longer the need to get involved with that sort of negative or abusive 'energy game' again.

I'm sure that Chrétien was well aware of the

VII. The Message of the Grail

Pandora's box that comes with every full-blooded relationship and I can only assume that he wanted to keep his manuscript down to a manageable size when he made his account of Perceval's relationship with Blanchfleur rather short and sweet. Admittedly, this was a bit of a cop-out but he had to get to the part about the Grail, so perhaps we can find it in our hearts to forgive him!

We are told that Perceval's encounter with Blanchfleur has affected him deeply. Through it he has been able to integrate the masculine Elemental energies in his psyche with the latent, hitherto hidden, feminine aspects of his being, but something else has also happened in the process. A meeting or marriage of energy polarities has occurred on the conscious level but his unconscious memories have also been activated. This is why he can't just stay and settle down with Blanchfleur. Something deep has been stirred up in his memory as he starts to think of home and the fact that he hasn't seen his mother for a long time.

Perceval remembers that when he last saw his mother, she was falling down in the entrance of her home and, apparently for the first time since he left home, he thinks of her and wonders how she is. This is, in fact, another of Chrétien's penetrating insights. As the heart opens up to more love, fears and other unresolved issues from the past are often remembered. From the spiritual perspective, they are meant to return into consciousness because this brings the possibility of

VII. The Message of the Grail

healing them. This 'blast from the past' is often confusing after the bliss of being with the beloved but Perceval knows that he must be honest with himself and he sets off again to retrace his steps and pay a visit to his mother. Poor Blanchfleur will have to wait!

The story's events start to become more complex and mysterious from now on, reflecting the truth of the real spiritual quest and the fact that some of the most profound breakthroughs or changes in spiritual consciousness are the result of the confusion of a crisis. Perceval sets off again with the intention of going home but he quickly loses his way in the forest. When he comes to a river, he can go no further because the water is flowing much too fast and the river is far too deep. He is frightened when he realises that he has no way of getting through or over the water.

The obvious suggestion of this symbolism is that Perceval must now face the full power of his previously unconscious emotions, this being one of the aspects of water's Elemental powers. He is suddenly confronted with this unknown function of his psyche. Somehow, he has managed to get through his life this far without giving his emotions a lot of attention so he is stopped in his tracks. Unprepared and frightened, he does not know what to do. (Has nothing changed in the archetypal male psyche in 800 years?)

Curiously, Perceval sees a fisherman, apparently completely at ease as he sits in his boat, calmly navigating the river's tumult. The fisherman gives Perceval

VII. The Message of the Grail

some guidance but this doesn't amount to much in terms of being a solution on a practical level. When it comes to facing the emotional depths of the unconscious mind, we may be lucky to have some support, but, in the end, we are on our own. Friends can offer to help but they can't do it for us.

Perceval does have the wit to follow the fisherman's instructions. He must change his direction and follow the line of the river rather than crossing it at this point. So, he climbs upstream, finds a cleft in the rock and eventually he looks down to see the Fisher King's manor house down in the valley below. The whole of this part of the story seems very dreamy. Later, we are told that when Perceval wakes up the next morning after staying the night in the manor house, everyone has gone and he is alone. I suspect that we are meant to infer that the whole episode comes in the form of a dream or an altered state of consciousness in the sense that it is spiritual guidance from a higher level of awareness which Perceval does not usually know how to connect with.

This does not belittle Perceval's experiences in any way. From the spiritual point of view, some of our most valuable information can be received in other than normal states of consciousness. It could be argued that this is, in fact, exactly where this kind of information always comes from. Chrétien actually suggests some beautiful clues that increase the chances of connecting with guidance from the 'higher' levels of our being.

VII. The Message of the Grail

Perceval must climb as he follows the river bank. The source of a river is always upstream so as Perceval climbs he is symbolically raising or heightening his emotional sensitivity as he moves towards the origin of the water's flow. As he shifts his awareness away from the mire and confusion of fear and emotional indulgence, he is moving to connect with the higher aspect of water's Elemental consciousness. This sensitivity has mysterious psychic abilities because it opens the door to his soul's intuitive wisdom which can offer him an understanding of the source of his problem.

At the top of the pathway there is a cleft in the rock that Perceval must pass through before he can look down into the valley. The path narrows down before he reaches the 'gateway' of this gap in the rock at the top. This is symbolic of him becoming more focused on looking for the source of the problem but the geography of his surroundings also hints that he is going to symbolically pass through a kind of birth canal before he emerges, reborn to a new perspective on the other side. When he passes through the cleft of rock, he is also looking down from a higher vantage point and this offers the promise of the overview of the situation. Perceval is going to be offered another angle, another way of viewing the problem that lies at the source or root of his unconscious fears and sense of disempowerment.

3. A Glimpse of the Grail

Perceval is welcomed when he reaches the manor house and the servants waste no time in taking him to see its owner, the wounded lord, inside. It is almost as if they all know that he is coming, the fisherman in the boat who gave directions being the same person as the Fisher King. Later, we find out that the wounded lord is the Fisher King and he is also Perceval's uncle, with the understanding that somehow there is a deep connection or relationship between the two men. There is also the inference that there is some kind of ancestral or collective issue that links Perceval's distress with whatever happened to cause the original wound from which the Fisher King is still suffering.

Chrétien does not discuss the nature and cause of the Fisher King's wound very much. This detail is another pivot of the story and it is consequently elaborated and embellished by other authors in later additions to the original text, but Chrétien tells us simply that the King was wounded in battle, that the wound will not heal and that this means that the King and his people continue to suffer because of it.

The Fisher King presents Perceval with a sword, saying that it is destined to be given to him. The symbol of the sword is traditionally associated with the air Element, representing here, amongst other things, the ability to use the 'higher' function of the intellect, spiritual insight, to provide a dispassionate clarity or overview that can create a greater awareness and more

VII. The Message of the Grail

information about the situation.

This particular Elemental power is singled out at this point in the story with the emphasis that the sword itself is special, that Perceval is meant to receive it and it is for him personally. The motif of the hero and his magical sword is common in many myths and legends, the story of young Arthur showing that he is the rightful king when he pulls the sword, Excalibur, from the stone being one of the most well-known examples.

The Elemental power of air is being singled out at this point for a reason. The 'higher' positive use of this Element offers the powers of seeing and communicating the truth with objectivity and clarity so Perceval is given this quality first so that he can understand the higher, spiritual vision of what he is going to be shown.

Perceval watches as a procession of young people walk past, carrying a series of mysterious and precious objects. First, there is a boy with a bleeding lance. The lance or spear represents the fire Element and the fact that it is bleeding suggests that there is something very strange about this particular Elemental power. The fire Element is shown distorted; its power is somehow operating in a manner that has become so destructive that it is causing bleeding, a clear demonstration of a wound. This obviously links back to the Fisher King's wound. In some later versions of the tale, the wound is actually described as being caused by a lance or spear that has pierced through the thighs of the Fisher King.

Two youths then come in, each one carrying a candelabra bearing ten candles. This detail is also

VII. The Message of the Grail

important. The numerology of this combination is 22 (10 + 10 + 2). Traditionally, in the ancient art of Pythagorean numerology, 22 is known as a 'destiny' or 'life path' number, having a powerful, spiritual significance. It was also linked with the 22 cards of the Major Arkana of the tarot, another pre-Christian teaching using the symbolism of the four Elemental powers that also has its origins in the Underworld Initiation and the mysteries of the Dark Goddess. Chrétien is at pains to underline the fact that even though his story has become rather mysterious and dreamy, he knows that he is offering the reader some important spiritual information at this crucial point in his tale.

Next, a girl comes in carrying a silver platter, sometimes called a trencher or serving dish. This is a symbol of the earth aspect of the Elemental powers. A platter is a large tray, often shown laden with fruit and other fine foods. In the ancient Greek and Roman traditions, the symbol of the cornucopia might have been used in this context to signify the riches of Mother Earth in all her material abundance, wealth and fertility. This symbol would have been too obviously pagan for the sensitive psyches of the Christian clergy of the time, so Chrétien chose the silver platter as the symbol of the potential abundance of the earth Element instead.

The final object that Perceval is shown is the Grail itself. This is described in terms that make it seem both fabulous and mysterious as it emits a wonderful light. In my understanding, this is Chrétien's chosen symbol of water, the Elemental power connected with the receptive,

VII. The Message of the Grail

emotional qualities of the feminine as they can be expressed in the mystic or the muse. The Grail can also be understood as a reference to the soul's consciousness, the inner source of the heart's power of unconditional love. The soul's essence embodies this very pure aspect of love that has no sense of personal attachment or desire for possession or control of the loved one.

So, what does this parade of objects signify? Perceval is being shown the importance of the powers of the four Elements, that they are of equal value in terms of their potential use and significance and that these powers are of vital importance in the spiritual journey. These are some of the key teachings of the Underworld Initiation. At this stage in Perceval's spiritual journey, he has already developed a considerable conscious mastery of the Elements of fire and air when he trained to be a knight with Gorneman. He then met Blanchfleur and fell in love with her. By being her champion, he actively demonstrated that he recognised and honoured the feminine qualities of earth and water when he protected her from persecution.

These two earlier episodes demonstrate Perceval's empowerment of the four Elemental powers on the conscious or outer, day-to-day level. He could have stopped at this point in his journey to settle down with Blanchfleur and live happily ever after but he didn't because his life path, usually called fate or destiny, the number 22, demanded something more from him when he remembered his mother and had the desire to go back to see if she was all right.

VII. The Message of the Grail

When he became lost in the forest and got stopped by the river, Perceval was encountering something emotionally distressing that had been hidden from his conscious awareness until that point. Then, when he was directed to the manor house of the Fisher King, he was shown the information and the spiritual tools, the powers of the four Elements, which will help him to sort out his problem – meaning, learning how to heal a wound that until now he did not know he had. In the process, he will begin the transformation of consciousness that was known as the Underworld Initiation of the Dark Goddess, the Underworld in this context being the process of learning how to consciously make a healing inner journey into the deep memory of what we now usually call the unconscious mind.

A further clue lies in the fact that the Fisher King personally gives Perceval the sword of truth, representing the 'higher' function or power of the air Element. This Elemental power is particularly singled out and Perceval can take it with him when he leaves the next day. The Fisher King is able to help Perceval as he passes on the destined sword that communicates spiritual insight and intellectual clarity. This will enable Perceval to gain the overview of his predicament as well as offering him a way of comprehending the spiritual transformation of consciousness that he is now engaged in. With this overview, Perceval is also shown that the fire Elemental power is bleeding and wounded, with the hint that the root of his wound therefore lies in the realm of the powers of the fire Element.

VII. The Message of the Grail

The power of the fire Element is the source of the energy behind creative action or initiative and, in its higher function, it also represents the power to make a judgement based on a sense of spiritual integrity, morality and personal conscience. This higher aspect of the fire Element represents the Fires of Purification of the spiritual conscience, the energy behind the sense of personal morality, which has the ability to judge right from wrong. The message behind Chrétien's symbol of the bleeding lance then becomes something along the lines of 'there is something out of balance with the way that you have been taught to make moral and spiritual judgements and this has caused a deep and incapacitating wound to the psyche on both the personal and collective level'.

When we find out later that the Fisher King is Perceval's uncle, we can infer that the energetic imbalance in the fire Element at the source of the original wound must be inherited in the sense that it is a cultural problem with an ancestral root. The development of all human culture and tradition depends on the process of handing down a myriad of complex habits, beliefs and conventions of behaviour from one generation to another. Many of these attitudes are instilled in us as we grow up because they are a part of the mindset or gestalt of the prevailing culture around us and while we may try to challenge them during adolescence, many modes of thinking become so deeply ingrained that they are rarely consciously confronted. Effectively, it is as though these beliefs and ways of doing things are inherited or

VII. The Message of the Grail

passed on in a way which is, for practical purposes, almost completely unconscious.

Some inherited beliefs or gestalts are positive or life-affirming but a surprising number are not. The rational part of the mind, functioning on the ordinary, day-to-day level with its logical thinking processes, rarely thinks to question or challenge the dogma of the status quo and it is easy to fall into a state of cultural mental inertia. When the Fisher King deliberately fastens the sword of truth onto Perceval, he is also saying, 'You must learn how to use your intellect to question, to seek out and find the truth'. Bringing this message into full consciousness is a vital key to changing any negative, inherited pattern of belief because such thought forms can only be transformed by first becoming consciously aware that they exist.

In the later additions to Chrétien's story, the bleeding lance is also clearly linked with the story of Christ's Crucifixion so there is another overlay to this part of the story which the Grail writers were trying to emphasise and communicate. When these legends were being written down, the Christian Church was becoming much more focused on having political control and spiritual power at the expense of the religious freedom of the individual. This adherence to spiritual dogma later became extreme, leading to all manner of persecutions and killings. In many ways, our patterns of thought and beliefs are still heavily influenced by this cultural inheritance as it continues to be passed on to reverberate in the psyche of the collective mind. I

VII. The Message of the Grail

believe that we are still fascinated by the Grail stories because we are still unconsciously aware of this Elemental wounding and we intuitively recognise the symbolic portrayal of the solution to the problem when we see it.

It has been suggested that the name, the Fisher King, was meant to be an encoded reference to Christ. At first, I could not make sense of this interpretation in terms of the rest of the story until I made the connection with Chrétien's message about the fire Element. Chrétien is using his story to comment on the emerging misuse or distortion of power that was starting to develop within the authoritarian, religious dogma of the Church's hierarchy and he observes that this is causing a deep sense of spiritual wounding that is beginning to affect everyone.

The character of the Fisher King represents an archetype of a male sovereign with considerable spiritual stature and wisdom and he seems to be patiently suffering his wound, acquired through no fault of his own. This symbolism only makes sense to me if Chrétien was trying to infer that it was the attitudes in the hierarchy of the Church itself that were responsible for the wound sustained by their King as they began to actively persecute the spiritual beliefs of other groups or sects, a gross distortion of the message of unconditional love and acceptance which their saviour had tried so hard to convey.

When Perceval sees the representations of the feminine Elemental polarity, earth and water, the silver

VII. The Message of the Grail

platter and the Grail, these symbols are shown intact. They are not damaged in any way but they do need to be recognised as being of equal value and power when it comes to understanding their combined use with the two masculine Elements so that a harmonious and healthy balance can be restored.

I find it fascinating that in the original story, the four Elemental sacred powers are shown on an equal basis but it is the Grail, the symbol of water, which later became the strongest mystical icon of hope that so many find particularly inspiring. Surely, this represents the intuitive understanding in every human heart that, as a symbol of unconditional love and spiritual acceptance, this is the vital ingredient that is needed to solve the issue of the inherited cultural and spiritual wounding that so many continue to bear.

Chrétien gives us another symbolic emphasis of the cultural wounding when he tells us that Perceval grows up in the Waste Forest. In some versions of the story, the Fisher King is defined as being the ruler of the wasteland with the implication that the state of Elemental imbalance is so extreme as to threaten the fertility and well-being of both the land and its people and that this situation must have been happening for some time to have resulted in the land being well on its way to becoming barren and infertile. The message here is that if the negative use of fire is not healed then the feminine powers cannot be equally honoured. The inner psyche is then made barren and the world around us also feels like a wasteland. How many massacres,

VII. The Message of the Grail

wars, polluted rivers and landmine-infested farmlands does it take before our rulers can understand this?

So, Perceval has been shown the source of his wounding. He is also given the key to beginning its resolution in the form of the four Elemental powers, with a particular focus for the time being on the sword of truth, a power which he can take away with him.

Perceval wanted to ask about the meaning of all that he has been shown but he remembered Gorneman's advice about keeping quiet and not asking too many questions. Where have we heard that one before? The fear of being punished for not knowing the answer is an important part of every authoritarian mindset of control because it uses shame, blame, criticism, ridicule, threat and punishment to intimidate, thus making it frightening to even question the deeper, spiritual truths of life. Unfortunately, Perceval has taken Gorneman's advice on board as he falls for another negative inherited indoctrination, hook, line and sinker. He cannot admit to not knowing something because he fears the censure of being the fool. He has been denied the spiritual understanding which only the holy idiot can use to see through lies to get to the truth.

I would like to thank Chrétien for his compassion at this point. He could have finished his story here. His hero has been shown the root cause of his wounding and he has been given both the spiritual wisdom and tools with which he can heal it. Chrétien used both his insight and understanding of the human condition when he decided to make his hero fallible. Like most people, Perceval is not able to fully comprehend the implications of seeing the truth of life at the first encounter. The weight of the emotional backlog of years of cultural conditioning is just too much. In today's terms we might say, 'He just couldn't get his head around it.'

Chrétien must have understood this human failing when he decided to continue his story. Perceval has been shown his gullibility but, in his frailty he is just like the rest of us, so, by making Perceval continue his journey, Chrétien was able to encode some more understandings in the rather convoluted events that happen next. Perceval has had a glimpse of the truth of life and, behind the scenes, his guiding soul will make sure that he does not forget it.

4. Redeeming the Past

The next morning, Perceval wakes up alone and rather confused. He wanted to ask about the meaning of what he was shown the previous evening but the house is now deserted and, with no one about, it seems as though he has completely missed his chance.

When he resumes his journey he has no clear idea about where he is going. He follows the trail of some fresh tracks and is led to the maiden who is crying over the body of her dead lover. When the maiden asks Perceval where he has come from and he explains about the manor house nearby, she scolds him for not asking about the wonders that he was shown. She explains that much good would have come about if he

VII. The Message of the Grail

had only asked about the meaning of the mysterious objects and that if he had asked about them, the Fisher King, his people and all of his lands would have been healed and restored to fertility.

This information offers more clues that suggest the source of the wound is both personal and collective. In the pre-Christian, Celtic tradition, the four Elemental powers were known as the four hallows, 'hallow' meaning 'sacred'. There was also the concept of sovereignty, the idea that a ruling king had a sacred, energetic connection or engagement with his lands and people. Every rightful or lawful ruler went through a ritual of ceremonial marriage to the 'sovereign' goddess of his landscape, a symbol of the feminine Elemental powers that governed the fertility of the people, the animals and the crops. This meant that if the character of the king himself became out of balance or wounded in terms of his relationship with the feminine principle, then the Goddess, sovereignty, would respond by withdrawing her input, bringing famine or war to his kingdom.

When this information is added to an understanding of the ways that the Elemental powers operate on both the inner and the outer levels of manifestation, we are led to the conclusion that the Celts understood that the king of a domain had two aspects of responsibility, an inner one and outer one. He had to take care of his personal sense of emotional harmony and spiritual integrity because the relative state of this inner balance was reflected in the dynamics of the outer conditions,

VII. The Message of the Grail

in this case, the fertility or abundance of his lands and the people around him. (This is one of the reasons why, in the myth of King Arthur, his kingdom starts to fall apart when his wife, the embodiment of his feminine polarity, falls in love and goes with another man.)

When the maiden makes a point of explaining about the Fisher King's wound and the effect that this is having on his lands and his people, I think that we are meant to infer that the root or source of Perceval's wound is a culturally inherited imbalance, something that affects the entire kingdom. This wounding has become so ingrained in the collective psyche that no one can escape it, though it can be healed by the individual on the personal level. If enough individuals heal by changing the negative pattern, then eventually, the whole of the society will change, but the individual, the king, must do it first.

In today's terms, this pervading state of cultural imbalance might be called something like 'the effects of centuries of a patriarchal social conditioning'. However, even though Perceval has been shown the answer, it was on the dream level and he was not fully conscious of what he had been shown. The maiden is trying desperately to wake him up so he can start to look in the right direction and consciously address the problem.

As Perceval's journey becomes rather confusing, the events of the next part of the story are more difficult to follow. When viewed from the purely rational level they become downright unlikely so we have to remember that from now on, Chrétien has moved out of left-

VII. The Message of the Grail

brain, male logic into right-brain, feminine feeling, intuitive perception, the soul aspects of Perceval's being. So, as if out of nowhere, the maiden tells Perceval who he is, that his mother died when he left home years before, that the Fisher King is his uncle and that she, herself, is actually his cousin who used to live with him and his mother when he was a young baby, which is why he can't remember her.

Not many people fixed in left-brain mode would believe all this information in a hurry. A few moments ago, when Perceval found her, the maiden was mourning a dead lover which she seems to have completely forgotten about now that she has clapped eyes on Perceval. Now she's his cousin and the Fisher King is his uncle. I know that it would be easy to throw in the towel at this point in the story with the conviction that Chrétien has now gone a bit nuts, but the part about the Grail was nice and perhaps there is a method in the apparent madness that is unfolding in front of our eyes? Hang on in there, I think there is.

Perceval had a spiritual revelation the night before, probably in the form of a dream or trancelike state. He still has the sword of spiritual insight that the Fisher King gave him, so he knows that something real has happened to him and that he hasn't made it all up. As he hangs onto his sword of truth, it starts to activate his intuition and his spiritual understanding. With an increasing clarity, he begins to cut through the layers of memory and time that have become an inherited fog of half-remembered events. Finally, he gets back to a

VII. The Message of the Grail

sense of his early childhood consciousness, a state of innocence when he was still able to connect his soul's consciousness. This is the part of him who always remembers the plans for his life's spiritual purpose and continues to be his guide, usually hidden behind the scenes. In the light of this new spiritual perspective, he then starts to review all the events of his past with a transformed insight and a new understanding.

The maiden represents another aspect of his inner feminine, the wisdom of his soul's intuition, something that Perceval has only partially glimpsed before. This mysterious focus of consciousness was with him when he was a small child but it became hidden beneath the increasing pressure and worries about day-to-day events as he got older. His soul continued to be there in the background of his awareness but when he left his childhood years behind, 'she' became elusive and more or less forgotten. So, for the first time in his adult life, Perceval consciously comes face to face with the personification of the spiritual consciousness that is the hidden source of his embodied life, the awareness of his 'maiden' soul. Of course his soul forgets about her dead lover when she meets Perceval. He was her lover who became 'dead' to her and here he is now, in front of her, conscious again of her presence. She knows that she can't waste the moment so, while she has got his attention, she has a go at him for being so forgetful, dumb and stupid!

Our soul can appear to us in many guises. We might prefer the mysterious and elusive dream lover or the

VII. The Message of the Grail

wise, supportive, infinitely loving mother, but she can also appear as the rather insistent, almost stern teacher if we are going off the rails and need to be reminded of our spiritual purpose. Our soul also embodies our sense of personal integrity, our feeling of having an inner reference point and the sense of having a moral conscience. Now that they are reconnected, Perceval's maiden soul must put on a show of being a bit of a shrew. She must make sure that he does not miss the real point of their encounter and she has got to alert him to some of his spiritual failings.

Perceval is fittingly contrite. He starts to understand how stupid, selfish and inconsiderate he has been in the past, particularly towards his gentle and selfless mother. He cannot, however, actually go back and ask for his mother's forgiveness. Understanding that she is now dead, he realises that this is now too late.

Chrétien has to be quite inventive at this point in his story because he has to demonstrate the fact that Perceval is remembering all the times when he went wrong in the past, particularly in his relationship with the feminine Elemental polarity as she was represented by his various earlier encounters with women.

Perceval sees all his errors as he realises there were times in the past when he went against the moral integrity of his soul's sense of right and wrong because of his egocentricity, selfishness, insensitivity or because of what he had thought was OK behaviour due to his cultural conditioning. When Chrétien gets Perceval to go after the knight who murdered the maiden's lover,

VII. The Message of the Grail

he is offering a shorthand way of saying that Perceval sees his errors and repents, now wanting to make amends for his selfish and inconsiderate behaviour towards women, the feminine, in the past.

In the next episode, Perceval encounters the girl he first met in the pavilion, right at the beginning of his quest. She is now dressed in rags as she is forced to ride in shame in front of her lover, the Jealous Knight. This 'blast from the past' offers Perceval a way in which he can redeem himself and directly make amends for an error that he made because of his earlier lack of spiritual understanding.

This incident demonstrates the fact that Perceval has learnt much from his past experiences and that he has resolved to change his behaviour. When Perceval duels with the Jealous Knight and wins, his sword is broken but it does not matter. He has made use of its insight and with this power he has been able to cut through to the root of the negative conditioning that he had inherited and unconsciously acted out. He has got the point of this lesson, so, as he makes amends, the sword breaks because it has done its job of making him more conscious and it is therefore no longer needed.

News of Perceval's chivalrous deeds of recompense get recognised by those around him. Perceval's whole relationship to life and others is changing. Even King Arthur is becoming aware of his gallant exploits and we are told that he sets out into the forest with his knights to find the noble Perceval.

Meanwhile, Perceval has resumed his journey,

VII. The Message of the Grail

unaware of impending fame. It has been snowing and when Perceval watches a hawk attacking a wild goose, some blood falls onto the ground. Perceval becomes entranced by the sight of the red blood on the white snow because it reminds him of Blanchfleur's white complexion and rosy cheeks. This means that when King Arthur arrives with his knights, Perceval is completely unaware of the presence of the other men.

This incident is typical of Chrétien's ability to encode layers of potent symbolism in a rather charming but apparently inconsequential episode. We are told that Perceval becomes entranced when he sees the red of the bird's blood on the snow. The obvious suggestion is that his consciousness has been shifted away from the ordinary level of reality by the impact of seeing the hawk's attack on the goose. The first layer of encoded information is therefore related to the way outer events can sometimes act as messages or triggers that activate previously unconscious aspects of the mind to induce profound experiences on the inner, spiritual level. Today we might call this a peak experience or supernatural encounter.

Seeing a hawk going after its prey when out and about in a forest may not be that unusual but hawks do not usually attack geese; they are much too big as a form of prey. So why does Chrétien draw our attention by specifying that the other bird was a goose? In many ancient traditions, birds are a symbol of the soul because both can fly, a symbol of leaving the physical body behind. In many Egyptian tomb paintings, the soul of the deceased was shown hovering above the mummified body in the form of a bird with a human head.

The hawk is also a symbol of the masculine, 'spiritual' polarity of the psyche with its ability to rise above and perceive the overview and hence gain clarity in a situation or problem. There is also the subtle link back to Horus, the Egyptian god of rebirth and new beginnings, who was also the son of Isis. The goose was a symbol of the 'fertility' of the soul, the intuitive, feminine attributes of the psyche. This legacy has come down to us through its associations with the magical qualities of Mother Goose, and there is also the message of riches or inner wealth, as in 'the goose that lays golden eggs'. In ancient Egypt, the egg of the goose was seen as a symbol of the cosmic egg from which the sun was birthed. Together, the symbols of the hawk and goose suggest the higher or soul aspects of the inner male and female energies of the psyche, usually symbolised as the sun and the moon.

This symbolism is reinforced when we are told that the red blood on the white snow reminds Perceval of his love for Blanchfleur. In many older teachings, the three feminine aspects of the creative principle were known as the Virgin, the Mother and the Crone. The Virgin symbolises the ability to conceive, the capacity to be a pure receptor or vessel for the creative 'spark' of the masculine polarity. The Mother represents the ability to nourish and nurture, to serve and take care of the child, the outcome or product of the conception.

VII. The Message of the Grail

The Crone symbolises the power of transformation so that, in apparent death, there is a transition or change that offers the potential for the new to be born.

White was associated with the purity of the Virgin aspect, so Chrétien makes sure that we know that it has been snowing. Even now we have the phrase 'pure as the driven snow'. Red was the colour associated with the Mother aspect of the feminine, hence the need to make a point of describing the redness of the goose's blood. Seeing the two colours together acts as a visual catalyst, helping Perceval make the inner spiritual connections between the masculine and feminine Elemental energies within his psyche. As he remembers Blanchfleur, the outer, physical embodiment of his own, inner 'other half', the feminine counterpart of his consciousness, he is able to fuse or marry the spiritual levels of his internal masculine and feminine energies to create new energetic connections and a higher level of spiritual understanding in his mind.

The colour symbolism of the three aspects of the Goddess is frequently encoded in myths and fairy tales. For example, in the story of Snow White, as a symbol of the persecuted feminine who has to be hidden until she is truly recognised and loved, Snow White is portrayed with fair, white skin, rosy red cheeks and lips and jet black hair. In Chrétien's story, the black aspect, the Crone, is missing at this point, another detail which will make more sense a bit later on as events unfold. At this stage in Perceval's inner process, from the colours that we are given, we can understand that Perceval's

VII. The Message of the Grail

inner masculine polarity has consciously accessed and successfully integrated the combined energies of the Virgin and the Mother aspects of the feminine polarity within his psyche. So far, he has not met up with the 'black' Crone aspect of the feminine, the 'Dark' Goddess; this encounter comes later.

When the King and his knights arrive, Perceval is still caught up in this inner encounter so he is completely unaware of what is happening around him. When Sir Kay tries to arouse him, Perceval unconsciously lashes out and Sir Kay breaks an arm as Perceval's blow knocks him down from his horse. This event acts like a form of retribution because Sir Kay was the knight who had mocked the psychic girl who had prophesied Perceval's future fame and achievements when he had first arrived at King Arthur's court at the beginning of his adventures. By inadvertently hitting the mocking and boorish Sir Kay, Perceval reveals that he can instinctively defend or champion the spiritually receptive qualities of the feminine consciousness that are at the source of the mysterious intuitive powers of the mystic and the muse.

This incident indirectly marks another crucial point in Perceval's inner journey and this is recognised symbolically when Perceval returns to his 'normal' state of consciousness to be greeted by the King and his knights. King Arthur is a kind of shadowy figure for most of the story but this time he makes a clear and definite appearance. Perceval's command of the Elemental powers have now evolved enough to function at a conscious level of awareness so he can

VII. The Message of the Grail

evaluate and abide by moral judgements which are based on his personal sense of conscience and integrity. This comes from his soul's level of awareness rather than from the self-centred focus of his ego.

The King appears in person at this point to signify that Perceval has now achieved a state of being in which he can consciously embody the positive qualities of both his masculine and feminine Elemental powers in equal measure. This is the 'commanding' level of spiritual achievement in the spiritual journey because it represents a real sense of personal sovereignty. It signifies the ability to consciously handle the four Elemental powers with balance, equality and personal integrity, both for the benefit of others as well as for the self. This is the outward sign of the genuine champion who has become the 'ruler' of self, someone who will no longer allow themselves to be swayed by the opinion or acts of others. (In the Major Arkana of the tarot, this stage in the spiritual journey is usually called 'The Chariot'.)

Perceval has worked hard to earn the acclaim that accompanies this turning point in his inner journey. In the story, it is suggested that he is still a young man but this level of spiritual awareness usually takes many years to attain and there is rightly a sense of victory or triumph that accompanies this inner achievement and personal success. This is represented in the story when Perceval's exploits are applauded and he is escorted back to King Arthur's court in triumph.

VII. The Message of the Grail

5. Meeting the Dark Goddess

In the interests of keeping up the pace of a good story, Chrétien does not allow Perceval to rest on his laurels for very long. With barely a pause for breath, the dark aspect of the Goddess turns up the next day in the form of a confrontation with the loathly lady or hag. Perceval is due to begin the Underworld Initiation in earnest, though he probably doesn't realise it. From now on, the essence of his journey will take place on the inner levels of his psyche and his consciousness will emerge transformed but, on the outer level, he will have to withdraw from other people as the details of his spiritual life become a mystery.

Who is the horrifying loathly lady? She was given various names in different versions of the story. Sometimes she was called the hideous hag or the bald damsel. In Wagner's interpretation of the story, Parsifal, she is called Kundry, a name derived from an old German word for folklore. Wagner makes Kundry an ambivalent character – sometimes she is ugly and frightening but she is also the beautiful maiden who is the bearer of the Grail.

All these names reflect the dark or the 'black', aspect of the Goddess, an embodiment of the transformative powers that are the third aspect of the feminine qualities of the psyche. In today's terms, she might be called the power of the unconscious mind as opposed to the conscious mind, which we would now call the ego. In Chrétien's time, she would have represented the wise

VII. The Message of the Grail

woman and the witch, someone who had learnt to navigate the inner realms of the unconscious mind to achieved the wisdom of her soul.

The Dark Goddess represents another level of initiation, the next spiritual challenge. Perceval has just achieved an inner victory, the conscious command of the powers of both the masculine and feminine qualities of the four Elements. He could have stopped there – many do. But if he wants to progress further and discover the secret of the Grail, he has to make a sacrifice. Why? In today's terms, in the story so far, Perceval has been working on the ego level of his consciousness. He has gradually acquired the many skills and abilities of the four Elemental powers on the conscious level. In doing so, he has been tested many times by being shown where he was using these powers negatively or destructively and every time he has managed to change his behaviour and discipline himself so that he now uses all these powers positively.

But (and this is a big 'but'), from the spiritual perspective, unknown to him, there are some aspects of the four Elemental energies that are still unconscious in his psyche. They are buried deeply in areas of his memory that have not been able to surface yet. If they do surface, he will have to risk letting himself fall apart on the conscious, ego level, so that any hidden, unconscious, negative 'energy loops' can be shattered, broken apart and reconfigured into new positive thoughts and beliefs. In effect, if he wants to go on with his spiritual quest, he will have to be willing to give up or surrender

VII. The Message of the Grail

all his ego powers and achievements that he has worked so hard to gain.

Psychotherapy now readily recognises some of the attributes or abilities that contribute to the qualities of the unconscious mind. This aspect of human awareness functions in ways which are introverted and receptive in relationship to the more extroverted, outwardly looking focus of the ego-mind. The unconscious mind has the power to remember more or less everything that has ever happened to us. This ability to remember and retain can be both a blessing and a curse so it was often symbolised in myths and fables as a woman who could behave like a fairy godmother one minute and an ugly hag the next. The ego-mind functions in a logical and linear way and the unconscious mind is based on the fluidity of the nuance of mood, feeling and impression. This means that the rational ego is quick to judge and dismiss the intuition when it arises from the deeper aspects of the psyche and, in the increasingly logical focus of our current culture, many people have come to fear or mistrust these non-logical powers of consciousness.

The unconscious mind also embraces the guidance of the soul's hidden level of awareness and Perceval's spiritual journey cannot be completed until this aspect of his consciousness is reclaimed or released from its secret 'imprisonment', a source of the damsel in distress imagery that became common in the mythic tales of the Middle Ages. In these stories, the maiden is often tied up and at the mercy of some kind of dragon or

VII. The Message of the Grail

monster, a symbolic representation of the repressed, negative, seemingly chaotic memories that also lie hidden in the depths of the unconscious mind. The powers of the innocent, 'maiden' soul can only be released into full consciousness when the fearful dragons of the past are faced and transformed, a fitting symbolism of the various processes of psychotherapy and emotional healing that many people are familiar with in the terminology of today.

The loathly lady seems to have it in for Perceval. She starts to curse and scold him because he was blessed with the opportunity of seeing the bleeding lance, the Holy Grail and the other mysterious treasures but he then omitted to ask about their significance. Perceval touched the forgotten secrets of life in his dreamlike vision in the manor of the Fisher King and his karmic soul, destiny, this time in the form of the loathly lady, will not allow him to forget it. Perceval realises that he must continue to look for the truth of life so he refuses to be sidetracked by the potential of an easy life of glamour at King Arthur's court and he makes a vow that he will not rest until he finds the house of the Fisher King again. Determined to discover the secret of the Grail, he sets out again on his quest.

Chrétien tells us that Perceval spends the next five years wandering alone in the Waste Forest searching for the illusive Grail in the house of the Fisher King. He has made a vow to discover the meaning of this ancient secret and he will not rest until he finds it. It is a lonely time. He has to face his inner demons alone and

VII. The Message of the Grail

Chrétien, quite rightly, cannot explain exactly how this is done through the symbolism of his story.

One spiritual understanding is reflected in the fact that Perceval must wander for a long time, tormented by the memory of his vision but unable to resolve its message. We are often given a glimpse of the truth of our purpose, perhaps piercing the veil of illusion for a brief time through the deep experience of love, only to lose it again and face the pain of thinking that we will never recover its inspiration. These dark nights are times of spiritual testing. The soul must make sure that we will not abuse her awesome power when we rediscover her so she has to stand back and allow the unconscious impurities of the self-centred aspects of the ego to be refined in the fires of inner torment, the cauldron of the Dark Mother.

We do not yet have a precise way of explaining how this inner mystery of the transformation of the psyche happens in spite of the development of psychotherapy and psychoanalysis. The unconscious mind and the guiding soul communicate through symbol, metaphor and image in a language that lies beyond the rational ego-mind, but Chrétien's imagery of Perceval wandering alone in the forest is a fitting way of describing the strangeness of this inner process. This stage of his journey is made up of the apparent confusion, fruitlessness, pain of purification and inner distillation that creates the alchemy of emotional healing. This takes a long time; it is highly personal and it cannot be related logically. Describing this stage of Perceval's journey as a time lost to inner wandering, aimless and unable to

VII. The Message of the Grail

see the wood for the trees in a forest, is a simple but accurate metaphor.

Perceval needs time alone because he must also release the subtle energetic ties that limit his ways of thinking and bind his emotional habits of behaviour to prescribed patterns of social convention. As we grow up, we have to learn how to fit into our family, our culture and our social tradition because physical survival actually depends on it. An abandoned baby will die; it has no way of caring for itself on its own. Unknowingly, we all understand the need to fit in, or 'tow the party line', as we start to imbibe the subtle rules, laws and limits of social convention almost from the moment that we are born.

Normally, these deep layers of conditioning and social protocol are rarely questioned. This part of the mind operates at a deeply unconscious level and is not usually available to scrutiny. It contains the most fundamental programming of our computer-like ego-mind so it has operating systems that function along the lines of, 'Well, I've always done it like that so why change now', 'If I risk confronting that, I'll die', or 'That's just the way it is, so don't rock the boat'. Perceval is being forced to confront all of these kinds of assumptions about the ways that he experiences and operates in his world because these patterns of very early conditioning are now 'up for grabs' – they have become conscious. His need to spiritually expand the ways that he looks at things is forcing him to ask: Why? Why? Why?

In today's world, we may be faced with this kind of inner questioning when something shocking happens to us. Perhaps everything in our life seems to be OK and then we suddenly lose our job, a loved one or our health. In the emotional turmoil that follows, it can be hard to understand that we will eventually emerge spiritually stronger for the experience as the fundamental structures of our lives are shattered and the carpet is dragged out from underneath our feet. To others, Perceval might appear the madman or the idiot but there is a method hidden in this kind of spiritual chaos.

6. Transformation and Rebirth

There are many layers of past fear, pain and loss that lie hidden in the memory of the unconscious mind and persistence is needed when it comes to trawling through the muddy sediment that lies at the bottom of the personal and ancestral memories of the psyche. In this solitary time, the rules and laws that contribute to the ties of social convention are broken as all the deep fears of abandonment or loss are faced and lived through. When we meet Perceval again after five years, he has lost all sense of time and he has forgotten what he was looking for in the wilderness of his inner journey.

Without realising it, Perceval actually arrives at the right place. He has been confronting and releasing all his hidden fears and with this done, he has come back to the innocent heart and the open mind that he once

VII. The Message of the Grail

had as a child. He has even lost sight of the object of his search. This is another spiritual truth. The subtle desire of looking for something can act like a cloud in the clarity of the truly innocent mind. Towards the end of the inner journey, the consciousness of the ego-mind becomes completely surrendered, having been forced to abandon its secrete agendas, social aims and hidden ambitions.

Perceval meets a group of knights and their ladies as they return from their pilgrimage to the chapel of a holy hermit. It is as if his story has come full circle. It had been a meeting with knights in the forest many years before that had first fired his ambitions and launched his original journey. In this last part of Chrétien's story, he tells us very clearly that it is Good Friday. This is significant because it references Perceval's final inner processes of spiritual alchemy with the crisis of transformation that Christ endured during the three days that began with Crucifixion and ended with the Resurrection on Easter Sunday.

When Perceval finds the hermit, he falls to his knees and weeps as he pours out the whole of his long story. This could be understood as a form of confession. Perceval feels the need to be forgiven and absolved of all the things that he still feels he has done wrong in his life. He had missed the chance to ask about the Holy Grail and he continues to feel responsible for the fact that he has not been able to find the house of the Fisher King again. He has still got a pattern of 'beating himself up'!

VII. The Message of the Grail

The hermit does not give him any form of punishment. Instead, the hermit explains that Perceval was not able to ask about the Holy Grail because he was held back by his unconscious sorrow about his mother's death. The hermit also tells Perceval that they are related and that the Fisher King is also a relative – his uncle.

Here, we are being given some more insights into the working of the unconscious mind and how an emotion that is persistently denied or ignored can continue to influence our lives even though we may not be consciously aware of it. The ancestral, social or family roots of the problem are referenced again with the fact that the hermit, the Fisher King and Perceval are all related to each other. The implication is that these inherited patterns and behaviours can be resolved but this can only be done if there is the willingness to become fully conscious of the issue and in the process, surrender to releasing all the past emotion that is bound up with it, even when it was not even 'your fault'. This is hard for the rational mind to understand because it does not make logical sense. Deep feelings of acceptance, surrender and forgiveness are needed so that emotional pain can be released even though the rational mind can't make any sense of it or understand where it is coming from. At the point of final reckoning, the past is the past and the understanding comes that we always did our best, whatever the circumstances, as did everyone else.

As if to emphasise this point, Chrétien tells us that the hermit's information causes Perceval to weep some

VII. The Message of the Grail

more and that he cries for a long time. This is a real 'let go' and I am sure that we are meant to assume that Perceval's ability to cry and let go of the past, together with the forgiveness that the hermit offers, is an essential part of Perceval's experience of healing.

Later, Perceval hears Mass, receives the sacraments and then rests. This seems to be the end of Perceval's story and the rest of Chrétien's text turns to the adventures of Gawain, another of the Grail Knights. As I suggested at the end of my adaptation of the story, it could be that this is essentially the culmination of Perceval's story because Chrétien clearly makes the symbolic link with Christ's Passion and the Resurrection. The story of Christ's Crucifixion, his three days of 'incubation' in the tomb and then His Resurrection or rebirth, could be seen as an archetypal account of the ritual of the Underworld Initiation itself, the climax of the inner process of enlightenment of consciousness that was the goal of the teachings of the Underworld tradition.

I like to think that Perceval actually perceived the spiritual truth symbolised by the Holy Grail at the end of his three days of 'incubation', resting in the 'tomb' of the hermit's chapel. I am sure that on the third day, Easter Sunday, he awoke to a new and transformed awareness and that he then experienced a sense of rebirth as all of his painful phantoms were finally laid to rest.

VIII. The Alchemy of the Four Elements in the Psyche

WE ARE ACTUALLY USING THE POWERS OF THE FOUR Elements all day, every day, in our daily life routines and experiences, but this is normally happening at a level at which we are not conscious. There can, however, be a profound transformation of awareness if the various functions of these powers are brought into a state of growing consciousness application and understanding.

These archetypal powers or energies enable our human consciousness, as the incarnating soul, to function with the three-dimensional existence of physical matter. The Elements act as the invisible medium or agents of the processes of creating physical substance or events so, in a sense, we are all like apprentice magicians, learning how to consciously and lovingly manifest our spiritual creativity through the medium of these four Elemental powers.

When the energetic qualities of the four Elements are understood and applied, there is the ability to completely change the ways that you interact with other people and the world around you. This information offers you a way of sorting out every aspect of your life, your relationships, career, health and creativity, as well as providing you with a way of understanding and consciously working with your spiritual pathway and your life purpose.

A conscious relationship with these powers demonstrates the truth that the ordinary incidents of daily life are a fundamental aspect of every spiritual journey and that there is no separation between the mundane and the sacred. The dynamics of every situation and relationship can then become a part of the spiritual quest. When knowledge of the functions of the four Elements is added to the understanding of reincarnation, these powers can then be understood as the agents of the process of gradually learning how to become sovereign of self and spiritual self-mastery is assured.

I found that the easiest way of learning how I was using the various Elemental powers was to use astrology to work out how these qualities were manifesting in my personality. The tradition in astrology is that the Elements of earth and water are seen as having the 'negative' feminine qualities of being receptive, passive and reflective whereas fire and air are understood to have 'positive' masculine, reactive, outgoing, action-based energies.

Incidentally, in most traditions, this male/female dynamic was understood to be at the essence of all creative processes. It was understood that there were always two polarities at work, a 'male' energetic polarity and a 'female' polarity that acted together to create

VIII. The Alchemy of the Four Elements in the Psyche

matter. This was probably most clearly expressed in the idea of yin and yang in the Chinese tradition but it is inherent to every teaching in some form or another.

In astrology, each of the twelve signs of the zodiac is seen as being under the ruling or governance of one of the four Elements. In this context, these powers act like four archetypal energies which then become modified or coloured by the constellation of stars in a given area of the heavens, the zodiac. A further overlay or influence is provided by the various positions of the planets at the time of birth. This gives the individual soul the basic template or configuration of cosmic energies that will influence the psyche and play out as the energies and attitudes of the personality of the current lifetime, as well as providing the mechanism for triggering the timing of the unfolding of events that will become the sequence of life lessons as they occur.

We are each, of course, unique, in both our soul essence and our life path, but an accurate astrology chart, drawn up for the time and place of birth, will provide a good indication of the particular balance of Elemental energies that an individual is learning to work with in the current lifetime. Many people have an emphasis of one or two Elements in their astrological chart, and these are usually the qualities that are easy or natural for them to access or use. The powers and energies of these Elements can be so instinctive that the abilities associated with them can give rise to innate talents or gifts in these areas.

The qualities associated with the Elements that have

VIII. The Alchemy of the Four Elements in the Psyche

less of an emphasis in the birth chart will have to be worked on or consciously developed through the various challenges that are a part of the complex processes of learning as we grow up. For example, at school, a child with an 'airy' astrological chart is likely to enjoy English literature or the facts and figures of science and mathematics but he or she may be reluctant to play a sport. In contrast, the 'earthy' child usually enjoys the rough and tumble of physical exertion and may see the time spent in a maths lesson as some kind of torture or penance.

One of the pioneers of modern psychotherapy, C G Jung, became very interested in astrology and he began to use it as a psychological tool to help him in his work with his clients. It is very likely that his definitions of the personality types owe much to his knowledge of the four Elements in astrology because they bear a remarkable similarity to both the Greek and Mediaeval concepts of the four humours or temperaments, aspects of the Greek understanding of the four Elements.

A core thesis in Jung's work was the postulation that there were a number of archetypal or primary motivating agents at work in the human psyche. He suggested that these energies were universal principles because he found that their motifs, symbols and themes were common to everyone in many different cultures, on both the individual as well as the collective level. I believe that Jung's work continues to be so influential because he had actually made the link that reconnects

VIII. The Alchemy of the Four Elements in the Psyche

the wisdom of the ancient teachings of the four Elements with the outlook of the modern mind.

Jung defined four personality types, these being sensation, feeling, intuition and thinking. He saw sensation as the capacity to receive information through the five physical senses: sight, touch, hearing, taste and smell. These are all sensations coming from the sense receptors of the physical body, the earthy aspect of human perception. Feeling can be seen as the process of evaluating input through the 'watery', fluid, receptive, emotional-body response. Intuition may be understood as the process of knowing directly from 'spirit', the vitality, action aspect of the fire Element. Thinking then becomes the process evaluating logical information and the mental processes of creating wordy communication, working through the airy function of thought.

Jung may have had another understanding about the ways that the four Elements function in the human psyche when he gave us the psychotherapy terms, extrovert and introvert. Extrovert personalities are seen to function in ways that are outwardly orientated; they are sociable and keen to spend time actively engaging with other people. Introverts are more inward-looking in the sense of being interested in the subjective, 'inner' realms of feeling, sensation and emotion. The introvert and extrovert qualities of the psyche reflect the basic feminine and masculine energy dynamic of human consciousness, which is comparable to the yin and yang energy polarity of the ancient Chinese system of thought.

VIII. The Alchemy of the Four Elements in the Psyche

When the qualities of the four Elements are linked with understandings of astrology[11] on the psychological level, fire and air can be interpreted as having 'masculine' powers, being more active, dynamic and outgoing. In contrast, earth and water have qualities that make them more 'feminine', that is, they are more receptive, responsive and inward looking. The polarity of behavioural definition between the two systems, astrology and Jungian, is striking, to say the least!

It is also known that Jung became very interested in the study of alchemy in the later part of his life and that he acquired copies of various old alchemical texts and manuscripts. The whole of the theory and practice of the ancient art of alchemy was based on trying to explain the processes of purification and transformation of the four Elements so they could be brought into a new state of being and balance. This outer alchemical process was understood to reflect the inner processes of the changes in consciousness that would ultimately result in an inner spiritual transformation or change in awareness that would then give a comprehension of the state of consciousness that became known as the 'Philosopher's Stone' or the 'Elixir of Life'.

With the knowledge that the Elements of earth and water function with a feminine polarity and that those of fire and air are correspondingly masculine, it is easy to see how these two sets of qualities give us the basic or typical stereotype of the energy exchanges that

---

[11] *Astrology, Psychology and the Four Elements* by Stephen Arroyo, published by CRCS, 1975.

underlie the traditional roles and relationship dynamics which commonly occur between men and women. When it is understood that the ultimate spiritual aim of every individual is to become completely balanced in terms of consciously using the powers of all the four Elements in an equal and harmonious way, it will be seen that relationships can be used consciously to learn more about our opposite function or Elemental polarity through the mirroring that is given by the other person in the dynamic.

The Twelve Signs of the Zodiac in Terms of the four Elements

Those born when the sun is in Taurus, Virgo or Capricorn are earthy, introverted people who take pleasure in the disciplines of the practicalities of life. They are very aware of their natural environment and have strong focus on the physical sensations that give them pleasure or enjoyment of their surroundings.

Cancer, Scorpio and Pisces people are also introverts. They have an acute, responsive sensitivity to the watery, emotional nuances and exchanges of feelings that occur between people in relationships as well a highly evolved, aesthetic appreciation and desire for beauty.

Aries, Leo and Sagittarius are extrovert fire signs. This means that they function with an active, vital, enthusiastic and dynamic kind of energy, which is always ready for some kind of creative action or new initiative. They are natural leaders who enjoy being 'out there, leading the pack'.

VIII. The Alchemy of the Four Elements in the Psyche

Gemini, Libra and Aquarius are also extroverts. They are governed by the Element of air, and they are more interested in intellectual pursuits, conversation with other people and communication generally. They are also good with facts and figures, enjoying the exchange of new ideas or concepts.

IX. Inanna's Journey into the Underworld
Breakdown to Breakthrough

THERE ARE SEVERAL VERSIONS OF THE ORIGINAL Sumerian story of Inanna meeting with her sister Ereshkigal. One of the best translations is in the book, *Inanna – Queen of Heaven and Earth* by Diane Wolkstein and Samuel Noah Kramer.

Inanna is already a powerful woman. In the land of the living, she is a mother, a queen and a priestess in the ancient kingdom of Sumer. As a mature woman, she decides to make a journey into the Underworld, the domain of her sister, Ereshkigal. As the queen of the Underworld realms, Ereshkigal rules 'the great below' with the Annuaki, the judges of the Underworld, deciding the fate of those who have just died as they pass through her kingdom before they are reborn into the land of the living.

In this ancient text, we are not given many details about the nature of the Underworld. The writer probably assumed that the reader would already know about this already so there would be no need to explain the details. The Underworld, however, was a common concept in many of the ancient traditions so it is easy to

IX. Inanna's Journey into the Underworld

get some sense of how it was viewed by piecing together information from the myths and legends of other cultures.

Traditionally, the Underworld was seen as the domain of the newly deceased so it was usually seen as a place to be feared. In modern terms, it could be seen as representing the many 'inner' realms of the subconscious, the unconscious and the super-conscious aspects of the mind. Every time that we shift our awareness away from the usual, rational, worldly, day-to-day focus, we are, in effect, moving into one of the 'other' realms of perception and experience, which belong to the non-physical, under-the-world realities that are also a natural part of the breadth of human consciousness. When we remember a vivid dream, we are bringing subconscious information 'up' into our conscious awareness so that we can then decode its message.

There are many realms or different levels that make up this other-world and Inanna's inner journey takes her far beyond the areas that she has already learned to navigate. In effect, in the course of her experience, Inanna learns how to go 'deeper' and 'higher' than she has ever gone before. In many of the older traditions there were systematic ceremonies, rituals and levels of spiritual teaching that led up to the Underworld Initiation. The sequence of events in the story of Inanna's journey reveals the stages of this inner spiritual process and the changes in consciousness that happen to her as a result.

IX. Inanna's Journey into the Underworld

Inanna understands that her journey is potentially dangerous so she asks her servant, Ninshubar, to promise to get help for her if she does not return after three days. Inanna also prepares herself carefully. She puts on all her special clothes, her royal jewellery and the other symbols of her current spiritual status, her worldly achievements and her power. At the entrance of the Underworld she is stopped by the guardian, who asks her why she wants to go in. Inanna says that it is because she wants to witness the funeral rites of the recently deceased husband of her elder sister, Ereshkigal.

Ereshkigal allows Inanna to enter the Underworld on one condition, that she remove one item of her royal regalia and clothes at each of the seven gateways. This means that after the seventh gate, Inanna is completely naked, gradually stripped bare of all her worldly protections and symbols of power. When Inanna goes into the throne room to meet Ereshkigal, she must bow down low to the Underworld Queen and the judges. Her sister, Ereshkigal, does not appear to be very welcoming. Ereshkigal glares at Inanna with the 'look of the Eye of Death'. She then speaks the 'Word of Wrath', utters the 'Cry of Guilt' and, finally, strikes her. Inanna apparently dies in this process. Corpselike, her lifeless body is hung on a hook jutting out from the wall, like a piece of rotting meat.

Three days and three nights pass and Inanna does not return. Ninshubar, her faithful servant, starts to raise the alarm. At first, no one is very interested or bothered that Inanna has been gone for three days in

IX. Inanna's Journey into the Underworld

the Underworld and that she might be dead. The 'father' gods, Nanna and Enlil, refuse to help, saying that Inanna was foolish to go in the first place and that she deserves all that she gets!

Finally, the god of water, Enki, agrees to help. He cannot go down into the Underworld himself so he scrapes some dirt out from underneath his fingernails and magically fashions two Elemental beings. He gives each Elemental, a gift to carry. One carries the gift of the 'water of life', the other carries the gift of the 'food of life'. Enki tells the Elementals to slip into the Underworld without being seen and then to join Ereshkigal as she mourns the death of her husband. Enki knows that Ereshkigal will be pleased by this show of concern and that she will offer the Elementals a gift for their kindness. At this point, the Elementals must refuse the offer of Ereshkigal's gift. They must say that they want only the corpse of Inanna. When they receive Inanna's corpse, they must then revive her by sprinkling the gifts of the water of life and the food of life over her body.

Everything goes according to plan. Inanna is 'reborn' as Enki's gifts restore her to life and she gets ready to return home to her family, lands and kingdom. As she leaves, she is confronted by the Underworld judges. Normally, no one leaves the Underworld alive, at least in a physical form; spirits can come and go but Inanna's journey is unusual and the judges are rather concerned. They decree that two 'galla' or Underworld demons, must go back with Inanna. The galla are given the job of finding someone to take Inanna's place in the

IX. Inanna's Journey into the Underworld

Underworld so that the Divine Order between the ordinary world and the Underworld is not upset.

When Inanna returns home, she quickly finds out who her true friends and family are. Her servant, Ninshubar, is delighted to find her alive and they hug each other as they are reunited. Her sons are covered in sackcloth and ashes, grieving the loss of their mother. The galla are still looking for their Underworld replacement but Inanna defends her servant and sons against their challenges, saying that all these people are loyal to her and love her, so they cannot be taken away from her.

It is a different story when Inanna returns to her palace. She finds that her husband, Dumuzi, has betrayed her. He has already taken over her position and throne and he is not even mourning her loss! Inanna wastes no time. She authorises the galla to take him to the Underworld but Dumuzi tries to escape into the desert where his sister attempts to help him. In some versions of the story an agreement is made whereby Dumuzi has to stay in the Underworld for six months of the year and his sister has to be there for the other six months. In other versions, Dumuzi is lost to the Underworld for ever.

At the end of her journey, Inanna has earned the right to use the powers of the Underworld mysteries of death and rebirth. She is now a goddess of the three aspects of the feminine powers, those of the Virgin, the Mother and the Crone, having encountered and navigated the mysteries of heaven, earth and the Underworld.

X. Inanna's Keys to the Underworld

1. The Desire to Know the Truth

THE DECISION TO ENTER THE UNDERWORLD REALMS, THE other than normal levels of human awareness, may be made consciously or unconsciously. Inanna consciously decides to go. She is already a powerful and accomplished woman. She is a wife and mother, and she has also trained as priestess so that she can take part in the religious rituals in the temples of her realm. On top of this, she is also the queen of her country, a ruler who has learned the various skills needed to govern her people. We can therefore assume that she has a great deal of knowledge as well as the experience of all the worldly aspects of life that would be available to her. Inanna makes a conscious decision to make the journey because she wants to add the spiritual powers of the Underworld to the many aspects of her more worldly expertise.

In the reality of today, this kind of Underworld journey might be represented, for example, in deciding to do a guided visualisation, a meditation, a Shamanic journey, or a past life regression. These are all ways of

X. Inanna's Keys to the Underworld

finding a way to shift the focus of the conscious mind so that information can be gained from the subconscious aspects of our being. Dream images and symbols also represent information from subconscious levels of our psyche and these can be actively re-engaged with when we return to a waking consciousness so that we can bring more understanding to their message.

In many myths and legends, the shift in awareness from the ordinary, daily level to the 'other-world' was often symbolised by the need to pass through a gateway or a door. The gateway to the Underworld represents opening up the deeper aspects of the unconscious mind so this was usually carefully guarded because it was something that the unwary traveller would normally wish to avoid! Some aspects of the unconscious memories of the mind can be unsettling because they contain fears from the past, so it helps if the traveller is prepared by knowing what they are likely to face!

In the normal process of growing up, we all develop a self-conscious aspect of the psyche, a part that keeps an outwardly looking focus that continually monitors ourselves, especially in relationship to other people. In psychotherapy terms this part of human awareness is usually called the 'ego'.

The ego functions as a kind of highly sophisticated, mental communication system that links learnt, physical and emotional experience with habitual patterns of thought or belief. This part of our mind learns from all the many kinds of situations that happen as we are

X. Inanna's Keys to the Underworld

growing up because this is its function. In many ways, it becomes like an extremely sophisticated onboard computer through which we gradually learn how to operate in the world around us so that we can survive.

Sometimes we learn from beneficial situations that have positive, creative outcomes. These kinds of events will have positive memories connected with them, which will be stored in the ego's 'computer' memory as a positive belief. For example, 'I like going to Grandma's because she welcomes me and offers me nice things to eat.' Other learning situations may not be so happy. If there was a fearful or painful outcome then the memory of the event creates a corresponding negative belief. For example, 'I'm not going to try at maths any more because the teacher made me look stupid when I didn't know how to do it.' Negative beliefs always involve a fearful, angry or painful emotional memory of some kind.

All of the ego's beliefs are meant to help in our survival – it makes sense to try to put yourself in positive situations and avoid negative ones! (Once was enough, why do it again!) The problem is that we live as social creatures and we must learn how be a part of the highly complex relationship interactions that happen all the time around us.

As children, we also learn a lot about how to survive in life from the culture that surrounds us as we grow up. We learn how men and women relate to each other from watching our parents and the other adults around us. A huge amount of play in childhood is about

X. Inanna's Keys to the Underworld

practising these social rituals, patterns and games before we have any real understanding of what they all mean. By the time that we are adults, we have all created a highly complex ego structure that is based on a myriad of sometimes conflicting beliefs. These have been forged from both private, personal experiences plus an overlay of beliefs that are inherited or passed on from the combination of the beliefs learnt from family, friends and the general culture around us. We then forget how we came to have all these beliefs in the first place!

We have to create this complex ego structure as we grow up. The ego is not just learning to survive, it is also the mechanism through which we gradually become empowered through the process of learning itself. We all have to acquire many kinds of skills before we can function as a successful and creative adult. This is emphasised symbolically in Inanna's story when it is stated that Inanna is a queen, priestess, mother and wife. In the culture of her time, Inanna had learnt all the skills that were needed so that she could function as a mother running a household, managing her own, corporate business and also preaching in the church on Sundays. Inanna was the first woman in history to publicly juggle all the skills of motherhood with the demands of the corporate ladder and still find time to go to a yoga or meditation class!

There is, however, a catch to having a strong and, at times, an over-powerful ego. As our psyche becomes more mature and we have created a level of success in

X. Inanna's Keys to the Underworld

the world, the need for spiritual reconnection starts to make itself felt. The first stage of our lives is meant to be about becoming empowered on the ego's level of awareness but, in this process, the soul's focus of consciousness usually becomes more or less hidden and 'buried' in the unconscious mind because the ego's focus is outward, towards the world and other people around us. Also, in time, the complex belief system of the negative ego, being still based on unresolved fears and painful memories of childhood, becomes a kind of energetic limitation or restriction when it is related to the higher, expanded perspective of the soul's level of consciousness.

On the spiritual level, the mental mechanism of the ego is supposed to have the role of communicator, acting as the agent or function that links the 'animal' perceptions of the physical body with the presence of the incarnated soul consciousness or higher self within. In the tradition of the ancient Greeks, this function was symbolised by the god, Mercury, who had the role of being the messenger of the gods. As a symbol of the soul's guidance, Mercury represents the communicating link that transmits the spiritual overview of a situation to the ego's aspect of consciousness. The ego in then supposed to translate the soul's message into a practical strategy for daily life.

Unfortunately, the ego aspect of the mind has a tendency to become overdeveloped, seeing itself as the master of the ship rather than the servant of the soul. Our Western culture has also taught us that in order to survive in a socially competitive world, we must learn to focus on a self-centred kind of existence that seems to be continually based on some kind of struggle.

As we grow up and learn the complex ego survival strategies, we don't realise that these behaviours are actually based on layers of fear and anger that come from the sense of having to fight or compete. Without understanding what is happening, by the time that we are adults, we have all developed a number of highly sophisticated emotional control patterns, 'power trips', that we habitually use in all of our relationships as our ego competes with the egos of others in various games of manipulation, control and counter control. In our modern societies, nearly everyone's ego has become so strong and noisy in its need to assert itself that it has forgotten that there is still an inner voice of the soul, whose spiritual purpose it is actually supposed to be serving! This is why some spiritual teachings talk about the need to 'drop' or 'move beyond the ego' because a strong, negative and stubborn ego can become a big hindrance to the spiritual growth of the soul.

The negative ego-mind thinks in ways that are very tricky and clever. It spends most of its time worrying about the future, deliberating about the past or calculating selfish outcomes in which it thinks that it can come off best. Without realising it, many of our relationships are based on these sorts of competitive ego games rather than the unconditional love and clarity of the soul's level of consciousness that we all still secretly dream of.

X. Inanna's Keys to the Underworld

This problem is rooted in the fact that the ego cannot actually comprehend unconditional love. Because the ego operates in logical terms, it makes love a rational exchange based on surviving, a case of 'If I do this for you, will you do that for me and then we'll automatically live happily ever after, won't we?' When, on occasion, the true unconditional love of the soul actually does manage to break through the ego's complex defence system, the ego does its best to talk itself out of the experience of love. Have you ever listened to yourself arguing that the feeling for the man who you have just been smitten with is stupid, ridiculous or soppy, as your ego tries to deny or suppress a power that it does not know how to control?

This means that, at some point or another, a greater comprehension of the soul's consciousness can only be achieved when there is a willingness to move past or beyond the ego's approach or outlook on life. Real spiritual growth can only happen when there is a willingness to move past or beyond the ego's fears, games and manipulations.

For this to happen, the ego's negative structures and beliefs have to be 'dismantled', taken apart, rearranged and transformed so that a 'rebirth' into a genuinely heart-based, loving, soul-focused level of consciousness can become possible. This is what Inanna wants. This is why she decides to make her inner journey into the depths of her unconscious mind. It will make her more powerful but not with the power of her ego. Her ego has been developed enough already through all the worldly experiences that she has already had. Her new power will come from an inner freedom founded on the unconditional love that comes from her soul.

2. The Courage to Face the Unknown

When Inanna comes to the entrance of the Underworld, she has to ask for permission to enter. If we are consciously wanting to access the deeper levels of our awareness, the timing of the journey has to be agreed on the soul level of our being and we may be denied access until the time is right. This function of the soul's consciousness is represented in the story when Inanna is challenged by the guardian of the Underworld.

There is a subtle but enlightening message in the related meanings of the words 'guard' and 'guardian'. The frameworks, gestalts and ambitions of the ego-mind function like computer programming that has to be dismantled and re-framed each time we need to embrace a deeper understanding of the spiritual truths of life but, as this is actually happening, we temporarily lose the energy shields that normally protect us from the verbal energy 'barbs' of others. At such times, the soul's spiritual overview of our life path guides us through this process, working in the role of the guardian who protects us in times of extreme vulnerability.

The game plan of the ego-mind is focused on survival so it tries to protect its interests as it resists change and concentrates on keeping control. This part of our awareness feels threatened when it begins to realise that it may have to let go of some of its strategies and games so

X. Inanna's Keys to the Underworld

feelings or thoughts of madness are common as the ego constructs and controls are broken down or shattered in the face of the light of the newly emerging, higher levels of awareness. This process can feel like a kind of nervous breakdown and the soul must carefully orchestrate the timing, guiding the process so that the ego-mind is not completely overwhelmed and pushed too far, too fast.

We get a hint that Inanna will go through a change of consciousness as she comes to the gateway to the Underworld. Ancient temples and sacred buildings were purposefully designed with a knowledge of sacred geometry so that colour, shape and symbolic forms created a space that would support a shift in consciousness away from a worldly awareness into the more expanded perception of the soul's vision. The word 'entrance' literally means 'to en-trance' or shift awareness. It is still possible to experience this effect in many buildings, especially those dedicated to religion or spirituality.

Humility is an important aspect of any spiritual journey because when we ask for more love and truth in our lives, this change might not come immediately or in a way that we are expecting it. The negative ego has to surrender its stranglehold on the psyche but it rarely gives up without a fight. Sometimes we are shown the entrance to the Underworld suddenly, apparently without any warning, perhaps in the shock of an accident, illness or a bereavement. Try to welcome these changes as openings to new possibilities, clouds that have silver linings that will reveal a greater spiritual perception. Sometimes we must go through a real breakdown before we can breakthrough.

The negative ego can also be very tricky. Humility can also mean that we may have to be alert to the fact that a spiritual search can also become a 'glamorous' journey with a hidden agenda for more spiritual power, which can be used to become more 'special' or 'important' in some way. This could have been a part of Inanna's motivation for her journey but we will never know for sure!

3. The Seven Gates of the Transition – Letting Go the Go Through

Inanna spends a lot of time preparing herself for her Underworld journey. She dresses in her special clothes and jewellery. These are all symbols of her social status and her powers as Queen and Priestess. Inanna is 'power dressing', perhaps hoping that a display of her worldly prestige and position will impress her mysterious elder sister, Ereshkigal.

Ereshkigal, literally, comes from another place. She is not interested in the kind of power that relates to worldly status or family inheritance so she decides that Inanna can only enter the Underworld if she is prepared to take off all the layers of her clothing, jewellery and other royal regalia as she passes through the seven gates. From the text, it seems that Inanna is somewhat surprised by this request, but she has the grace to comply. Dutifully, Inanna does a kind of forerunner of the dance of the seven veils as she is forced to relinquish her costly apparel to become as naked as the day she was born.

These details are, of course, highly symbolic. We often forget that our clothes do not have the pure function of protecting us against the weather, keeping us warm when it is cold or cool when it is hot. They may offer physical protection but they also symbolise the complexities of the ways that we think and feel about ourselves, especially in relationship to others. The newspaper gossip columns would be seriously short of copy if there was a ban on writing about what the film stars were last seen wearing at the latest fashionable event.

Clothes function as a symbolic, psychological and visual message that expresses how we see ourselves as well as projecting what we wish to show about ourselves to other members of our society or group. Just think for a moment about the implications of the phrases in common use such as 'dressed to kill', 'power dressing', 'dress code', 'formal dress' and 'badge of office'. Often, without even thinking about it, our clothes become extensions of our ego, they speak volumes and we are usually very, very attached to them! They are a kind of complex visual, symbolic and social communication system with deep psychological implications, and as such, they are intimate 'tools' of the ego in its determination to project itself and generally make itself felt.

Clothes and make-up are also about social defence. Many women who habitually wear make-up will refuse to go out of the house until they have had time to 'put their face on'. Men will not enter an important business meeting without a tie and suit, armouring themselves

X. Inanna's Keys to the Underworld

from the verbal attack of others. How many public employees feel that they are somehow protected from the sometimes rather unpleasant duties of office when they are able to wear a uniform? Even Adam and Eve were forced to make do with fig leaves rather than run around in nothing at all!

In her wisdom, Ereshkigal knows that if Inanna wants to receive the full experience of the Underworld Initiation, she must be willing to allow herself to become as naked and vulnerable as possible, physically on the outside and psychologically on the inside. This suggests that in making Inanna remove her clothing and jewels, Ereshkigal's insight was that this would be a symbolic peeling away of Inanna's ego-mind as the layers of protection were surrendered one by one. Inanna's psyche needs to return to a state of childlike innocence and purity, bare of the complex masks and protections of her ego's proud defence structure. She must be willing to dismantle all her layers of learnt controls and negative beliefs that have been a part of her socially prescribed behaviour before she can experience the spiritual truths of Ereshkigal's Underworld domain.

The seven gates that Inanna passes through could be understood to represent the most important energy centres of the spiritual aspect of the body – the seven chakras. The term 'chakra' comes from the ancient Sanskrit word meaning a vortex or spinning wheel. This describes the way that the chakras operate as centres of subtle energy that connect the sensation input of the

X. Inanna's Keys to the Underworld

physical body with the other aspects of human experience – the emotional, mental and spiritual ways of perception. The soul's guiding consciousness uses the chakra energy system to coordinate the subtle flows of spiritual energy that are needed in the process of developing higher levels of consciousness or spiritual awareness.

Each of the seven chakras acts as a focus of consciousness through which we learn about a different 'arena' of life experience and these life arenas relate to the seven main areas of 'programming' that make up the circuits of the ego-mind's belief systems. This means that as Inanna surrenders the seven items that make up her clothing and jewellery, she is symbolically giving up all the ego controls and strategies that she has learnt over a lifetime as a mother, a priestess and a queen. This is not an easy thing to do but, in honouring Ereshkigal's request, Inanna is demonstrating that she is sincere in wanting to learn about the secret mysteries of the Underworld.

This process of dismantling the ego's structure is complex so it is coordinated by the soul's spiritual overview of the life journey. As Inanna complies with Ereshkigal's request and releases the protection of the layers of her jewellery and clothing, she is consciously doing her best to release all of the 'masks' of her ego's attachment, her pride in her worldly achievements and social position. She also demonstrates her willingness to surrender to experiencing a new way of being, a greater wisdom based on her soul's expanded level of consciousness. As she takes off her clothes and jewellery, Inanna realises that she must be willing to surrender all the worldly powers and abilities that have marked her out or made her somehow 'special' from the ego's point of view. In Ereshkigal's throne room, Inanna's worldly preferences will not be given any pride of place.

In the practicalities of modern life, the spiritual need to surrender the ego's protective masks may not be so obvious and the decision to enter the realms of the unconscious mind is not always in the form of careful ritual. Even so, the soul of our being has not forgotten us. The spiritual lessons of life are now more likely to come disguised in the day-to-day events that challenge our preconceived ideas and make us feel somehow vulnerable by removing a part of our 'support structures'. If we can learn how we can use these problems and losses, they can be 'reframed' and accepted as an opportunity for a new spiritual awareness. It is then possible to come closer to the vision of our soul, even when its guiding light is still mostly hidden from our view.

4. Facing the Mirror of the Dark – Breakdown to Breakthrough

After passing through the seven gateways, Inanna is completely naked as she enters the throne room and encounters Ereshkigal and the Underworld judges. She is completely unprepared for what happens next.

> Then Ereshkigal fastened on Inanna the Eye of Death.
> She spoke against her the Word of Wrath.
> She uttered against her the Cry of Guilt.
> She struck her.
> Inanna turned to a corpse.

X. Inanna's Keys to the Underworld

Inanna is already vulnerable so she cannot use the cleverness of her usual defences to deflect this apparently merciless onslaught. As she collapses, it looks as though Ereshkigal has killed her. How? What really happens?

Inanna has voluntarily given up all of her conscious 'ego games' on her way down into the Underworld. They were peeled off, layer by layer, as she undressed and took off her jewellery at each gateway. She has allowed herself to be vulnerable and defenceless, so she is in a state of complete spiritual surrender when she bows down to honour Ereshkigal and the judges but she has not realised that underneath her conscious ego games there are deeper layers of memory that are normally buried in the unconscious part of her mind. These deeper mental constructs and control frameworks must also be shattered and given up.

Ereshkigal has no time to spend on pleasantries. Instead, she cuts to the quick and attacks Inanna energetically, verbally and physically. She has to. Inanna's protective ego screens, masks or veils, are no longer in place and this means that Ereshkigal can strike out and hit all of Inanna's remaining ego 'attachments' with a devastating accuracy. Ereshkigal's attack forces all the remaining negative emotions and beliefs that have been very deeply repressed in Inanna's unconscious mind up into consciousness so that the last remnants of her ego's negative control patterns and structures can be 'killed', shattered or dismantled for good.

X. Inanna's Keys to the Underworld

Ereshkigal has a higher motive in mind and she can't afford to waste her chance. Before Inanna is able to stop her, Ereshkigal must work to shatter the last of Inanna's unconscious ego defences so that Inanna has the opportunity to realise her own soul's consciousness hidden within her. Ereshkigal can only do this through attack, she must be cruel to be kind, knowing from the higher perspective of the Underworld's spiritual perception that, at this moment in time, this is the most loving thing that she can do.

So why does Inanna collapse? Ereshkigal is highly intuitive and very wise. She attacks Inanna with the negative aspects of the four primary, Elemental qualities that energetically interweave through the interactions of relationships and the structure of the ego. Each blast of Ereshkigal's carefully focused energy hits a layer of Inanna's remaining unconscious ego structure and shatters it.

> The Eye of Death – air Element
> Word of Wrath – fire Element
> Cry of Guilt – water Element
> Physical Strike – earth Element

As the last parts of Inanna's ego are challenged, they break. As they shatter, this part of her psyche will die for good. Inanna will never be able to view her life from her old standpoints again.

Out of every cultural and family grouping evolves a kind of agreed set of patterns, habits and expressions of behaviour that is permitted or deemed acceptable.

X. Inanna's Keys to the Underworld

There is another set that is not acceptable – perhaps actually punished. Some of these patterns or traditions are passed down from one generation to another as each generation unconsciously agrees to play the family or ancestral 'game' and therefore, continue the tradition. These traditions include a range of permitted emotional responses as well as thoughts and beliefs. Any individual who tries to challenge these fundamental rules of behaviour is frowned upon or actively punished, something we are often willing to have a go at in adolescence, before 'settling down'.

When the individual is ready to grow on the spiritual level, a period of personal reflection or self-analysis starts to happen. This includes the process of mental and emotional questioning so that issues or negative experiences from the past can be resolved and healed. This naturally involves a kind of reappraisal or redefining of the individual's fundamental attitudes and beliefs. At first, this occurs on the personal levels of memory but as the deeper memories surface, another layer of past experience begins to come into consciousness, a layer that the psychotherapist, C J Jung, was the first to call the collective unconscious.

In my understanding, there is a part of the ego structure that originates from this collective level of human experience. At some point in the personal inner processes of spiritual growth and change, this deep level of the unconscious mind is encountered so that the influence of negative patterns of thinking and behaving, which have been unconsciously passed

X. Inanna's Keys to the Underworld

down from the ancestral levels of experience, can come up to be cleared.

We start to learn these patterns of thinking and behaving when we are very young under the normal circumstances of growing up. Some extremes of emotional feeling and passion may become feared, by both the individual and the collective psyche. As we grow up, we must all learn what is right and wrong from those around us. As children, we find out what is emotionally and behaviourally permissible and what is not. As the ego aspect of our consciousness develops, it learns how to act as a kind of judgmental 'agent' that controls the feeling aspects of our psyche. That is its job. We cannot interact as social animals without having some prescribed cultural patterns or 'agreed' rituals and routines. We must all learn how to understand so-called anti-social behaviour at some level!

From the spiritual perspective, the ego is meant to operate in a way that allows us to learn how to have conscious control of the animal awareness and instincts that are a natural part of our physical bodies. This means that it is important to develop the functions of ego control and discipline because they are obviously necessary as a vital aspect of growing up. The trouble is that some of the cultural traditions that every society has invented have also been designed by those in positions of authority to repress the creativity of the 'masses' so that they can be kept 'under control'.

Also, if the ego-mind has learnt how to become too judgmental, fear-based and rigid, it starts acting as a block by refusing to let in information that is trying to come in from the spiritual aspects of our being. In the maturity of life, even the structures of the collective unconscious aspect of the individual's ego-mind can become too repressive, negative, and limiting from the spiritual point of view.

A recent example of this level of collective consciousness being challenged on the group level was the sexual revolution in the 1960s when a whole generation of young people began to fight the highly restrictive social and religious dogma that was still a legacy from the Victorian morality of over sixty years before. Another example was the Women's Movement. When there are enough people willing to challenge the status quo, eventually this causes a lasting breakthrough in public opinion, the term popularly used as a summation of the collective prevailing attitudes and beliefs of the time.

5. Transformation – Marriage with the Soul's Integrity

In many cultures the butterfly is used as a symbol of spiritual transformation. Old routines and patterns of thinking and behaving must be dismantled before they can change, and this takes time. While the caterpillar is undergoing its process of metamorphosis it is very, very vulnerable. It needs to be cocooned, literally.

It is the same for Inanna. Her body is left for dead, hung on a hook, like meat left to cure. Inside herself, she is beginning an inner journey under the guidance of her soul. She must face the truth of her deeply repressed emotions, now released from the censor of the conventions of social habit, culture and training. She must see through all the lies and deceptions of the ego games and power trips that have been governing all of her relationships. The spiritual truth is demanded and only complete self-honesty will do as she is tested on every aspect of her emotional integrity.

She can only do this on her own. Everyone is suspect. She needs time to go back into her memory and acknowledge every situation in her past when, out of fear, she gave away the integrity of her emotional power to another person and she must vow to herself that she will never do this to herself again. She will also have to acknowledge every time that she tried to coerce another person into doing something that was against their will, and again, vow to herself that she will never try to influence in this way again.

She must also see that real love can only function as an aspect of the truth and that you cannot have one without the other. As she understands this, she will make a commitment to love, and in doing so, vow that she will never again try to manipulate out of fear or to gain power. All this takes time and she does not move as part of her dies and becomes transformed by this awesome change in her consciousness.

As she realises that she will now have to completely honour her love, her truth and her soul's integrity in all of her future interactions with other people, she understands that all of her relationships will be now be based on love and she will not want to connect with anyone who uses fear or control again.

Our negative ego develops as we grow up when we are judged by those around us. As children, we automatically learn how to judge or censor ourselves. As children, we also learn to judge our behaviour by watching the adults around us as we try to copy their behaviour and 'get it right'. We are also judged as good, bad, pretty or plain – the list is endless. All this learning acquired through judgement has become unconscious by the time that we are adults, but a voice in our heads still carries on judging, long after we have left home.

By deciding to learn about the Underworld realms of the unconscious aspects of the mind, Inanna has asked for the ultimate in spiritual growth, so Ereshkigal obliges her and delivers the complete package of these negative judgements wholesale, thereby killing the last, remaining aspects of Inanna's inherited social and collective ego.

6. Rebuild to Rebirth

Eventually, after a process of dismantling and clearing, it is as though Inanna's ego-mind is wiped clean. All the negative loops and patterns of thinking and believing have been broken apart into pieces and her ego-mind is innocent and open again.

All relationships are built on some kind of energy exchange, even if it is of the 'I'll do this, if you do that' level of interaction. Inanna has been giving up all her negative patterns of interaction and she does not want

X. Inanna's Keys to the Underworld

to play all the old games again when she returns to the land of the living, so something else has to happen first. She will not be looking for or depending on negative exchanges of energy anymore so she must therefore learn how to nourish and sustain herself with a spiritual energy instead.

When Inanna is revived with Enki's gifts, we get a bit more understanding about this new source of nourishment and what it might be. Enki's gifts are called the 'food of life' and the 'water of life'. We are also told that they are magical, which I presume means that they are not visible to ordinary eyesight. Food is an aspect of the earth Element, a product of the goddess of Mother Earth, which nourishes and sustains life. Water is also completely necessary for life. However, because they are called 'gifts', it suggests that we are meant to be looking at them in terms of forces or powers, rather than literal, physical gifts of food and drink.

With this in mind, I think that these enigmatic phrases are actually referring to the Elemental powers of earth and water. This suggests that Inanna has gained a new perception or understanding after her ordeal. She now has earned a command of the subtle, feminine Elemental energies of earth and water and these powers also have the ability to feed and sustain her in a new way because she is now fully conscious of them and how they function. This will give her a more inner, spiritual and self-reliant energy focus when she returns to her life in the land of the living.

A little bit more information can be gleaned from the

ancient Hindu tradition from India. The role of subtle, unseen energies is very much a part of this religion and many types are recognised. The body of planet earth is understood to be bathed in a kind of sea of vital, subtle energies, which interface with physical life and nourish it on an energetic level. Some of these subtle energies are seen as being related to the air that we breathe, so every time that we breathe in we are actually taking in this energy without being aware of it.

One of the best-known forms of this energy is called 'prana' and the Chinese have a similar concept that they call 'chi'. It seems possible to me that this could be a similar concept to the 'food of life'. So what is the water of life? If prana is the 'higher' food aspect of the earth Element, what is the higher aspect of the emotions of the water Element? None other than unconditional love!

7. Return and Revision – Walking Your Talk

When Inanna goes to leave the Underworld, the Annuaki, the Underworld judges, move to challenge her. In the normal course of events, nobody leaves the Underworld alive, that is, in a physical body. The judges are concerned about upsetting the balance of the natural order of things so they tell her that she cannot leave the Underworld 'unmarked' and that she must therefore take two Galla (furies or demons) with her as she leaves. They also tell her that because she is leaving the Underworld 'alive', someone else has to come into the Underworld to replace her and that the Galla will find the replacement.

X. Inanna's Keys to the Underworld

Inanna has experienced the truth of unconditional love in the Underworld and in this sense, she is 'marked'. Her consciousness has been transformed and she will look at everyone she meets with a new perception. She has to honour the changes in her consciousness after her inner journey so she can no longer play any ego control or manipulation games and she will not let others play them on her, either.

The Galla represent the alarming or frightening clarity of Inanna's new perceptions. Because Inanna has seen through the illusions and deceptions of all her own ego's power trips and games, she can now clearly see through any ego games that other people might be playing. She has become acutely aware of everyone's vices as well as their virtues and everyone's motive is transparent to her.

This new clarity of perception is represented by the Galla when Inanna returns home. The Galla waste no time in challenging each person that she encounters because they are still looking for a replacement for the Underworld. Inanna meets her servant, Ninshubar, and then her two sons. She can easily defend them against the Galla because it is perfectly clear that they love her and that they have her best interests at heart.

It is different with her husband, Dumuzi. He has betrayed her in her absence by usurping her throne. He has taken over her powers and position as Queen and he is not even mourning her loss! Suddenly Inanna realises that Dumuzi does not really love her. He does not even respect her as an equal. He is only interested

X. Inanna's Keys to the Underworld

in relating to her because of her social position and he is quick to take these for himself as soon as she is out of the way.

Inanna is very clear that she does not want to put up with this kind of relationship anymore. She is angry and makes no attempt to censor her feelings. She unleashes the full fury of her new emotional clarity onto Dumuzi in the same way that Ereshkigal had unleashed it onto her:

> Inanna fastened on Dumuzi the Eye of Death.
> She spoke against him the Word of Wrath.
> She uttered against him the Cry of Guilt.
> 'Take him! Take Dumuzi away!'

The Galla seize Dumuzi, beat him up and then attack him with axes. They have found their Underworld replacement! In this way, Inanna becomes fully empowered as a woman. She was already familiar with the powers of the Virgin and Mother aspects of the feminine polarity. Now she has completed her Underworld journey, she has become a 'wise woman', a Crone. She now has the inner authority to be able to wield, with clarity, the soul's powers of the Dark Goddess with love, truth, and spiritual judgement. She has also become sovereign of her self.